The Likeness is in the Looking

The Likeness is in the Looking

Collected Writings of Patrick George

Edited by
Susan Engledow

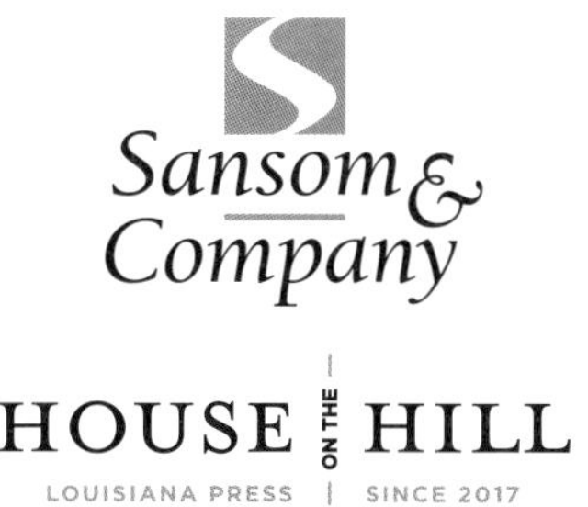

Sansom & Company

HOUSE ON THE HILL
LOUISIANA PRESS | SINCE 2017

First published in 2020 by Sansom and Company,
a publishing imprint of Redcliffe Press Ltd., 81G Pembroke Road, Bristol BS8 3EA
www.sansomandcompany.co.uk · info@sansomandcompany.co.uk

ISBN 978-1-911408-66-6

British Library Cataloguing-in-Publication Data
A catalogue record for this book is available from the British Library.

Copy-edited by Gemma Brace
Design and typesetting by E&P Design

Printed and bound in Wales by Zenith Media

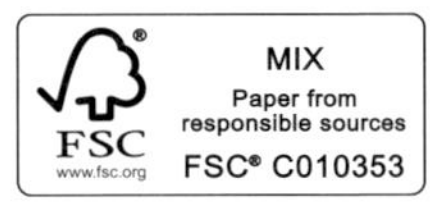

Front cover: *Portrait of Horatia and Claude* (detail), c.1986
Back cover: *Moreton Terrace Wallpaper* (detail), c.1968

CONTENTS

Foreword · 7
Susan Engledow

Introduction · 9
Christopher Moock

✦

A letter from Patrick George · 19

'Introduction' · 25

Painting what you can see from a single viewpoint · 31

Notes on painting · 41

Likeness · 57

Teaching notes · 91

✦

Acknowledgements · 133
Editor's note · 134
About the authors · 135
Patrick George · 136

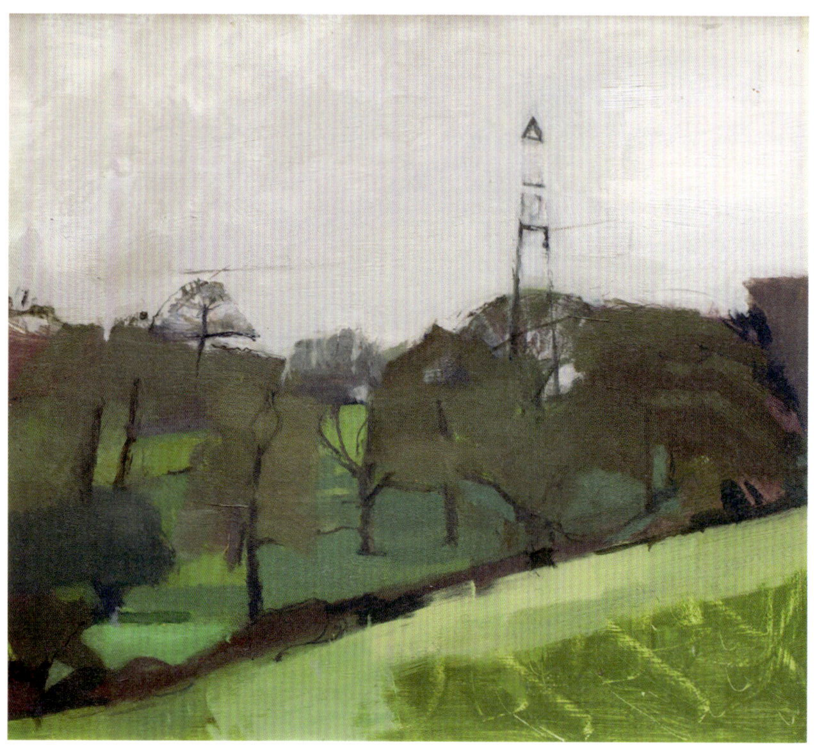

Hickbush towards Valley Farm   1960s · oil on wood ·42 x 45 cm

FOREWORD

Susan Engledow

THIS BOOK IS A COLLECTION OF WRITINGS BY PATRICK George, a highly respected artist and teacher at The Slade School of Fine Art, where he subsequently became Professor. The writing within is taken from various sources, some reproduced verbatim and others edited in order to make them more accessible.

A key source is his personal diary where Patrick recorded his thoughts about painting. Some of these notes were written whilst he was in the fields painting from the landscape. Another is his notes for a lecture, which he gave at The Slade on 'Likeness', in which he broadly discussed the subject with particular reference to painting from the model. Other sources include a catalogue introduction for *Drawings of People,* an exhibition which he curated for the Arts Council of Great Britain (1975); a letter published in the catalogue for the exhibition 'A Singular Vision: Paintings of the Figure by Contemporary British Artists' (1985), and an article for the magazine *Uppercase* published by his friend, the architect Theo Crosby, all of which have been reproduced in their original format.

The final source is Patrick's teaching notes, which span many years beginning in 1956 and continuing right up to the mid-1960s. Within these, I have pulled together his thoughts on what to teach, why he considered it important to teach these particular things, and how they relate to his own painting. I was extremely fortunate to have been taught by him, to have sat for him for many paintings, and to have been very close friends with him for most of my life. This relationship has given me some insight into the way he thought about art and putting together the different strands in this book has been an enormous privilege.

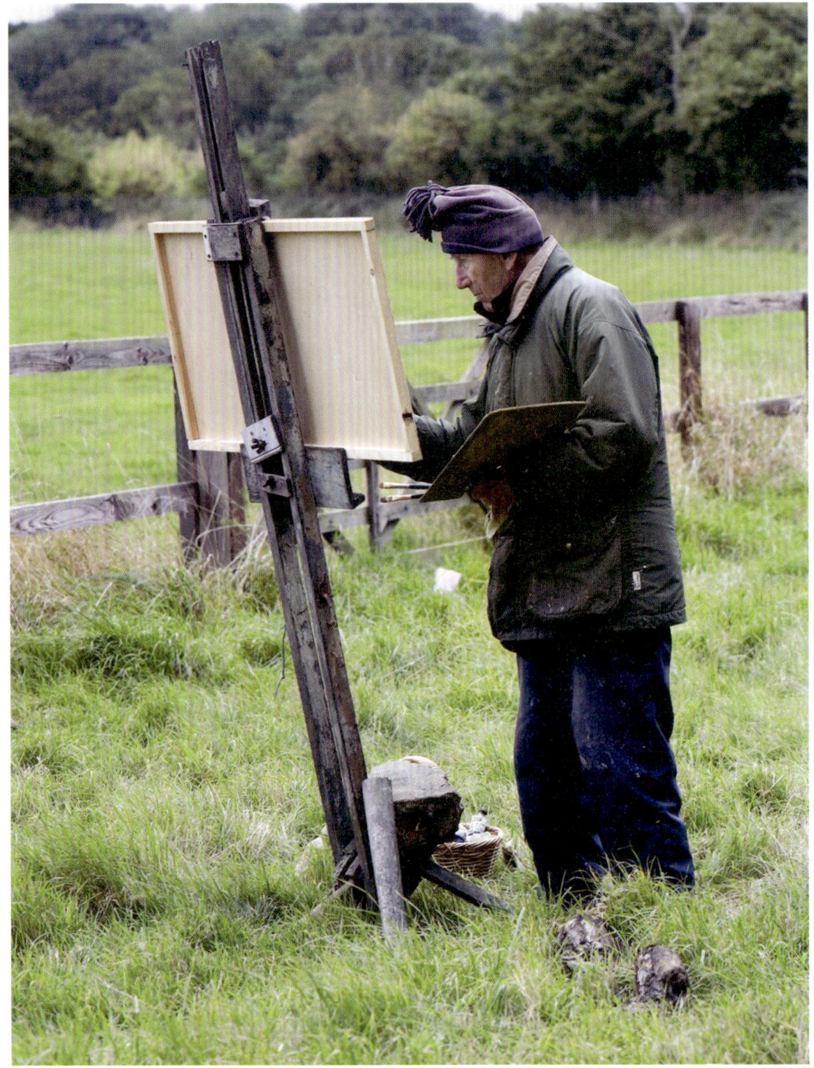

Painting in the Suffolk landscape, 2012 © Andrew Warrington

INTRODUCTION

Christopher Moock

PATRICK GEORGE (1923–2016) BEGAN HIS LECTURE ON 'Likeness' at The Slade School of Fine Art, in the late 1960s, with the unchallengeable observation that 'Lectures are made from words and paintings are not made from words'. Within this volume collecting his own writings on art this point alerts the reader to the special nature of these texts, in which, to quote again from the lecture 'I have tried to keep the words close to painting.' These quotes emphasise the priority given to the visual throughout, despite their sometimes surprisingly loquacious and speculative aspect.

Former students such as Tony Rothon have testified to George's inscrutable nature (even to his favoured students), indicating that words could be slow to emerge when art was the subject.[1] Susan Engledow, who came to know the mischievous playfulness of the private man is one who saw the full picture of his personality, within which his serious dedication to the practice and teaching of art were facets, albeit major ones. In all artists the relationship between personal character and the practice of art is a rich seam, of varying relevance, but undeniably present.[2] This is why an artist's writings are always of interest.

The public and the private man are seen together in this collection. These texts record two aspects of the artist's thought. First there are the previously published texts which introduce George's thoughts, engaging with an aspect of portraiture, with repeated references to key terms such as: 'change', 'appearance' and 'likeness'. These public concerns set the context for (and sit alongside) his own personal reflections, transcribed from handwritten notes. These concern his direct experience in the field, and bring home to us the arduous physical nature of his chosen and sustained practise of landscape painting. His observations

1. *Patrick George 28 July 1923–23 April 2016*, memorial booklet (London: Browse & Darby, 2016), pp. 8–9.
2. Rudolf and Margot Wittkower, *Born Under Saturn* (New York: W.W. Norton and Co., 1963).

on nature are interspersed with meditations on the masters of landscape painting. The second group of texts are specific to The Slade, where he spent his entire teaching career (almost 40 years). Connected with the initiation of his programme of weekly classes, these convey his ideas on art theory and perception, deriving from his own artistic practice. It is hard to imagine them being read out as short lectures at the start of a day's work. They perhaps were written (as Susan Engledow suggests) as part of the preparation for each week's teaching, and referred to, or elaborated upon at some point within the practical unfolding of each class. Presumably they were repeated, or adapted over the years. As well as elucidating George's own artistic philosophy, they reflect the post-war academic environment of this distinct and influential art school, within a secular, progressive academic institution, University College London (UCL).

Founded in 1871, The Slade had been associated from the late nineteenth century and into the twentieth with some of the major figures in the British art world including William Orpen, Percy Wyndham Lewis, Stanley Spencer, Augustus John, Gwen John, Spencer Gore, Harold Gilman, Mark Gertler, Dora Carrington and David Bomberg.[3] George's mentor, Sir William Coldstream (1908–1987) had enrolled as a student at The Slade in 1926, graduating in 1929. According to Charles Harrison 'Bloomsbury kept its eye on The Slade'[4] and notably Roger Fry, the key figure in introducing avant-garde French art to Britain lectured there. Vanessa Bell, Augustus John and Duncan Grant sponsored the Euston Road School (based in nearby 12 Fitzroy Street), which opened in 1937 with Coldstream as one of the founder members. By the time George arrived to teach at The Slade in 1949 (at Coldstream's invitation), Coldstream was Professor, having been supported in his application by Sir Kenneth Clark (later Lord Clark)[5] who had been introduced to Coldstream by Fry. Sir Lawrence Gowing (1918–1991), an ex-pupil of the Euston Road School succeeded Coldstream as Professor, and in turn, George took on the position from 1985 until his retirement in 1988. Many

---

3. www.ucl.ac.uk/slade/about/history [accessed 12 December 2019].
4. Charles Harrison, *English Art and Modernism 1900–1939* (New Haven and London: Yale University Press, 2nd edition, 1994), p. 66.
5. Bruce Laughton, *William Coldstream* (New Haven and London: Yale University Press, 2004), p. 156.

of George's teaching texts (published here for the first time) seem to articulate more fully ideas that were implicit in Coldstream's own approach as an artist. Of all the painters who Coldstream invited to teach, George seems to have been the closest to him in this respect.

As an ex-serviceman George had an air of authority. His bearing was upright. As I recall, he usually wore a black jumper and mustard yellow corduroy trousers. As for others of his generation, service in the Royal Navy in World War Two had been a formative experience for George.[6] Sharing rather basic accommodation in Lower Marsh, Waterloo, after the War, his early group of friends Myles Murphy, Anthony Eyton and Sir Christopher Pinsent recalled the sense of ship-shape order he required from them. Something of this brisk military manner comes across in the language of his teaching notes, some of which can seem like short commands – he says that students (his crew?) must follow his rules, even though it is a 'game' (mentioned in the lecture in relation to Coldstream and in the teaching notes). He sounds self-depreciating and ironic, but his words come with a confidence perhaps derived from his naval experience (he was second in command of a landing ship at the Normandy beaches on D-Day). The game of dispassionate observation, in making skilful and accurate distinctions, creating edges and depicting planes seems urgent, as though George had internalised similar skills from his time in the Navy and deployed these in a new, apparently unrelated, context.[7] After demob from the Navy, Camberwell School of Arts and The Slade were institutions, which in those days must have had much in common with the Navy, despite the obvious differences in purpose. The Slade itself – a grand, if austere building – could have been a naval college, or even a beached battleship washed up in Bloomsbury. Painting in the springtime countryside, George imagines that the electricity pylons in his field of vision resemble 'Nelson's ships in line'.

Unlike most art schools then, The Slade was part of an

---

6. Christopher Moock, *Patrick George: From Prose to Poetry*, exhibition catalogue (Colchester: The Minories Ballroom, Cobbold & Judd, 2018).
7. A precedent for this may be the case of the American painter James McNeill Whistler, who as a teenage cadet at West Point Military Academy in the nineteenth century had been trained in map making and surveying, see Daniel E. Sutherland, *Whistler: A Life for Art's Sake* (New Haven and London: Yale University Press, 2014), p. 26.

academic environment which must have encouraged George to consider his place in art history (in relation to the institution itself and beyond), referencing associated academic disciplines, as well as the collection of the National Gallery where he inspects and ranks artists of interest according to usefulness to his project.[8] In this he followed Coldstream who had advocated a wider engagement for The Slade within UCL, and Clark who had initiated a dual programme of promoting young British artists, and engaging them in a 'productive dialogue with the past.[9, 10] Frequent mentions are given by George to certain 'Old Masters'. As with Coldstream and Gowing he seems to be comfortable with the idea of being at the heart of the Establishment, making quite conventional artistic choices as his points of reference. On the other hand according to Bruce McLean, in later years George was irate at the suggestion that he could have become a Royal Academician, showing a distinction in George's mind between the enduring historical value of traditional art and the contemporary reactionary reality of the Royal Academy.[11, 12]

In his 'teaching notes' George says of The Slade that 'this school is perhaps most famous for its drawing', but his own ideas on the teaching of drawing were radically different to those of his predecessors.[13] When he states that 'these classes are entirely my concern' he explains that they reflect his own practice, in attempting to draw what he sees (despite the difficulties which he acknowledges in the opening diary of his own landscape painting). Gowing referred to this as 'subversive traditionalism'.[14] In his rather traditional Eurocentric artistic references, despite a period in Nigeria, George does not follow the broadened view of Roger Fry's *Last Lectures*, published posthumously in 1939, which presciently encompass an awareness with what would now be called World Art[15] (unlike, say Eduardo Paolozzi a student at The

8. Kenneth Clark had been the Director of the National Gallery from 1934–1945, and from 1948 Coldstream sat on its board of Trustees. Laughton, Ibid. p. 155.
9. Laughton, Ibid, p. 155.
10. Chris Stephens, 'Chapter 3: Patron and Collector' (especially p. 96) in Chris Stephens and John-Paul Stonard (eds), *Kenneth Clark: Looking for Civilization* (London: Tate Gallery Publishing, 2014).
11. Notes made from Professor Emeritus Bruce McLean, speaking at *Patrick George Remembered at The Slade*, 8 March 2017, Cruciform Lecture Theatre 1, University College London.
12. Coldstream had repeatedly rejected nominations to become a Royal Academician, see Peter T.J. Rumley, *William Coldstream*, catalogue raisonné (Bristol: Sansom & Co., 2018), p. 194.
13. Laughton, Ibid, p. 160.
14. Julia Fischel, *William Coldstream / Euan Uglow, Daises and Nudes*, exhibition catalogue (London: Piano Nobile, Robert Travers Works of Art Ltd., 2016), p. 5.

Slade from 1944–1947).[16] Nor does George's teaching relate to the parallel developments at Goldsmiths where psychoanalysis and 'anti-pedagogical' approaches chimed in with the anti-authoritarian mood of the 1960s.[17] Nevertheless, in retrospect from a post-war position, George might seem to fit the image of the coming 'pure painter' with his 'detached contemplation of shapes and colours' which Kenneth Clark (in his preface to *Last Lectures*)[18] anticipates as a response to the 'bloody fanaticism' of the late 1930s. Interestingly Clark sees the 1930s as comparable to the period in which Michel de Montaigne (one of George's favourite authors) 'achieved the perfect expression of scepticism and liberal curiosity', a phrase which could perhaps describe the character of George himself.[19]

Within the European context (which references to the National Gallery in George's writings show to be central to his aesthetics), Gowing characterised George as 'essentially a Northern painter' (he repeatedly likens him to both Pieter Brueghel the Elder and Peter Paul Rubens) in contrast to George's younger friend and colleague at The Slade Euan Uglow (1932–2000) who represented for Gowing the Italian tradition. Indeed Uglow became associated with Piero della Francesca,[20] however, it was Roger Fry who had begun the habit of likening the work of modern artists to him, by first comparing Cézanne to Piero.[21]

Gowing's idea had seemed insightful in the 1980s, but reading these texts by George we might assume that some of the concerns expressed in them were actually closer to the ideas of Uglow (for instance on mathematics and geometry). It is George however

---

15. David Summers, *Real Spaces: World Art History and the Rise of Western Modernism* (London: Phaidon Press, 2003) and Julian Bell, *Mirror of the World: A New History of Art* (London: Thames & Hudson, 2007).
16. Eduardo Paolozzi, *Lost Magic Kingdoms and Six Paper Moons*, exhibition catalogue (London: Museum of Mankind, British Museum Publications, 1985).
17. Beth Williamson, *Between Art Practice and Psychoanalysis Mid-Twentieth Century: Anton Ehrenzweig in Context* (Abingdon: Routledge, 2015), pp. 104–108.
18. Although Clark may have imagined Victor Pasmore in this role, see Kenneth Clark, *Another Part of the Wood, A Self-Portrait* (London: John Murray, 1974), p. 251.
19. Kenneth Clark, 'Preface' in Roger Fry, *Last Lectures* (Cambridge: Cambridge University Press, 1939), p. vi; Christopher Moock, *Patrick George: Recent Work*, exhibition catalogue (London: Browse & Darby, 2010), and Andrew Lambirth, *Patrick George* (Bristol: Sansom & Co., 2014).
20. Lawrence Gowing, *Patrick George: Paintings, Drawings 1937/1980*, exhibition catalogue (London: Arts Council of Great Britain, 1980); Catherine Lampert and Richard Kendall, *Euan Uglow the Complete Paintings*, catalogue raisonné (New Haven and London: Yale University Press, 2007), p. xxiii; and Christopher Moock, *Susan Engledow: The Principle of Tranquillity, paintings and drawings from 1985 to 2015*, exhibition catalogue (Spain: El Palacio de Congresos de Ronda, 2016).
21. Anna Greutzner Robins, *Modern Art in Britain 1910–1914* (London: Merrell Holberton Publishers, Barbican Art Gallery, 1997), p. 23. Influenced by Bernard Berenson, Fry had established himself as a specialist in Italian Renaissance art before his conversion to Modern art.

who articulates them and writes these quite elaborate and sometimes lengthy pieces. The two men shared ideas in regular discussions, and publishing George's own teaching notes here for the first time we can see that Gowing's broad opposition of their artistic characters is an oversimplification). George's notes contain extended references to Italian Renaissance art theory (citing Leon Battista Alberti, Piero della Francesca, Leonardo da Vinci and Andrea Palladio as well as Vitruvius) and cover topics such as geometry, perspective, representation of complex shapes in space, the picture plane and the grid, the Golden Mean, and proportions of canvases, etc. Such references may reflect the emphasis on Italian Renaissance art in the History of Art Department at UCL, which was linked to The Slade and the influence of Rudolf Wittkower in particular.[22] What may have appealed to George in Italian Renaissance treatises on art was their rationality as applied to artistic problems. Reason had also been an Enlightenment principle endorsed by the founders of UCL and in retrospect the mid-twentieth century could seem to be a period of optimistic consensus when it was still possible to believe in the power of Reason to make a better world, moving 'away from catastrophe and towards civility.'[23] George mentions Classical authors including Plato and Lucretius regarding theories of vision and several moderns are cited including Baudelaire, Mondrian, Le Corbusier and Kokoschka. The inclusion of Albrecht Dürer is worthy of comment, due to the strongly Latin/Francophile nature of Fry's influence on the British art world in the inter-war period[24] and the continuation of this tendency after World War Two. In the 1950s the influential art historian Bernard Berenson had also denigrated German art (including Dürer, whose paintings he said 'seldom exceed').[25] George's interest in Dürer is focussed on 'the grid', which shows Dürer at

22. Rudolf Wittkower, *Architectural Principles in the Age of Humanism* (London: Alec Tiranti Ltd., 1952), pp. 90–94 which George refers to. Wittkower's appointment as Professor of Art History at UCL in 1949 was supported by Coldstream. He was followed in this position by E.H. Gombrich. Laughton, Ibid. pp. 160–161 and 190.
23. Konrad H. Jarausch, *Out of Ashes, A New History of Europe in the Twentieth Century* (Princeton, New Jersey: Princeton University Press, 2015), p. 401.
24. Roger Fry, *Vision & Design* (London: Penguin Books, 1920), p. 163, and Emma Barker and Annabel Thomas 'Case Study 3: The Sainsbury Wing and Beyond the National Gallery Today' in Emma Barker (ed.), *Contemporary Cultures of Display* (New Haven and London: Yale University Press and London: Open University, 1999), pp. 79–81.
25. Bernard Berenson, *Piero della Francesca or the Ineloquent in Art* (London: Chapman & Hall, 1954), pp. 9, 13 and 14.

his most objective, and human proportions, which shows him at his most Italianate.[26] Although German (and thus excessively emotional according to Berenson) in this case George may have seen Dürer as conforming to his own type of painter, given the opposition he proposes between two distinct types of artist. In the letter from George (published in the catalogue for *A Singular Vision*, 1985) we read that some artists 'visually examine' the model, while others 'visually hug' the model. The examples he gives of these two types are Piero della Francesca and Rubens (one Italian and one Northern, perhaps confirming Gowing's distinction between Uglow and George). But despite his obvious 'Englishness' George seems not to wish to overtly introduce nationalism into his vision of art.[27] When interviewing him in 2010 I appreciated his fondness for Rubens[28] (a 'hugger'), but was surprised by his interest in Dürer. Knowing his fondness for Gainsborough and Constable[29] I had assumed that for him Englishness might have been more directly manifested in his art. However, returning to the Italian references (and to a more nuanced idea of artistic nationalism) it is interesting to note that by the mid-twentieth century there was a general belief within an influential circle that Piero della Francesca had assumed the status of an honorary Englishman, 'impassive, that is to say unemotional' according to Berenson.[30] In this context, George's detached type of artist is the one who 'visually examines' the model. He is the one who is discussed in the article in *Uppercase* magazine with his 'effort to see flat the three-dimensional object' and the one who practises measuring, which according to his diary he deploys in order to 'try to assuage my despair'. In this context the reference to Dürer's grid in George's lecture is

26. Erwin Panofsky, 'Chapter viii Dürer as a Theorist of Art' in *The Life and Art of Albrecht Dürer* (Princeton, New Jersey: Princeton University Press, 1955), especially pp. 260–267 for his 'Theory of Human Proportions'.
27. George's 'Englishness' is emphasized in Lambirth, Ibid, p. 165.
28. He had travelled to Belgium after the War to visit the location of the Flemish artist's Chateau du Steen on a bicycle.
29. Landscape painting has been seen as particularly close to national identity. 'Constable never visited Italy' but he 'loved his country' according to Nikolaus Pevsner, *The Englishness of English Art* (Harmondsworth: Penguin Books, first edition 1956, 1978), p. 157.
30. Albert Boime, 'Piero and the Two Cultures' in Marilyn Aronberg Lavin (ed.), *Piero della Francesca and his Legacy, Studies in the History of Art No. 48* (Hanover: University Press of New England, 1995), especially, pp. 259–260. Before World War One the art promoter F.R. Marinetti had powerfully critiqued the contradictory aspects of English identity in relation to both personality and artistic tendencies, as seen from an Italian perspective. He castigated both the Royal Academy and the N.E.A.C. from an avant-garde perspective, see L. Rainey, C. Poggi, and L. Whitman (eds), *Futurism, An Anthology* (New Haven and London: Yale University Press, 2009), pp. 70–74 and 197–8.

understandable as a physical barrier, suggesting the picture plane, and distancing the painter from his subject, and thus no longer linked to excessive German emotionalism.[31] In fact George suggests that a later Northern painter 'the father of self-expression Van Gogh' (1853–1890) employed the grid exactly as such a physical corrective to precisely these innate and potentially troubling Northern tendencies.[32] Perhaps George's message here and in his teaching notes is that all artists have to balance self-expression with detachment. This certainly seems to have been the case for an Italian contemporary of Van Gogh who also used the grid, the quietly dramatic (and now rather obscure) Italian painter Antonio Mancini (1852–1930), whom John Singer Sargent had called 'the greatest living painter'.[33]

The three artists chosen by George in the section on 'Three Painters' in his lecture, Frank Auerbach (b. 1931), Coldstream and Uglow all taught together at The Slade. If the above realignment (in the light of their relationship to the old masters) can be considered correct we may also consider that the latter two shared George's position. Auerbach by contrast is approved of even though his work is obviously not distanced. In fact George refers to 'touch' (perhaps echoing Berenson's idea of 'tactile values').[34] Auerbach is a 'remaker' (emphasising the physical aspect of making) rather than a distant observer.

Because George represents an empirical rather than theoretical strand of art practise emphasising the search for likeness as a goal at the end of his lecture (and was certainly no Royal Academician as mentioned above), his opening words in the lecture perhaps

31. Later in the lecture Dürer is also invoked in relation to Uglow's concerns with measuring and proportion.
32. Northern Expressionism is contrasted to Italian Classicism in Herbert Read, *The Meaning of Art* (Harmondsworth: Penguin Books, 1931), pp. 87–8.
33. Ronald Alley, *Tate Gallery Catalogues: The foreign paintings, drawings and sculptures* (London: Tate Gallery, 1959), pp. 132-5 and Thomas Bodkin, *Hugh Lane and his Pictures* (Dublin: The Arts Council, 1956).
34. Bernard Berenson, *The Italian Painters of the Renaissance* (London: Phaidon Press, 1952), pp. 40–46.
35. Giovanni Pietro Bellori, in A.S. Wohl, H. Wohl, and T. Montanari (eds), *The Lives of the Modern Painters, Sculptors and Architects* (Cambridge: Cambridge University Press, 2005), p. 77. The Carracci ran an influential Academy in Bologna, but Annibale is presented as more interested in practise than theory. Carl Goldstein, *Visual Fact over Verbal Fiction* (Cambridge: Cambridge University Press 1988), pp. 10–13.
36. It is perhaps counterintuitive to associate George with Reynolds rather than Gainsborough, although it may be helpful as a corrective to the picture, which he paints of himself as a countryman despite the fact that he actually split his time between London and the country. According to Maureen Lea Connett although he is the Head of The Slade in London, 'Patrick regards himself as a country worker, living his days outside in the fields like one of the animals' in 'A painter noted in his field', *The Countryman*, Summer 1986, pp. 77–82.
37. Conversation with Susan Engledow, 13 December 2019.
38. Sir Joshua Reynolds, in Robert R. Wark (ed.), *Discourses on Art* (New Haven and London: Yale University Press, 2nd edition, 1997). Reynolds' language of persuasion to his students includes such phrases as: 'I wish you to understand.' and 'I wish you to be persuaded' etc., pp. 79 and 117.

fortuitously echo those of earlier painters within the teaching context. Several hundred years previously Annibale Carracci had claimed that 'poets paint with words, painters speak with their works.'[35] In an illuminating passage praising Auerbach, George rather surprisingly quotes Sir Joshua Reynolds (who in the eighteenth century also drew his inspiration from Italy) and his advocacy of the 'Grand Manner'.[36] (Reynolds here is promoting the search for broad effects rather than fussy detail.) Reynolds himself had used his knowledge of Italian and Northern art to advocate for contemporary art practice in Britain. Although this is his only reference to Reynolds, George was fond of reading his *Discourses on Art* and they seem significant in relation to the tone of George's own writings.[37] Reading *Discourses* one is aware of an ongoing effort to engage and direct the practice of his students through the employment of frequent references to Italian precedents.[38] Like Reynolds, George's instructions are also urgent and confident, but his concerns are more practical. They bring us closer to the man himself, and encapsulate his own concerns as an artist, as a few final statements extracted from his notes demonstrate:

'To-day I wish to make clear what I mean by <u>accuracy</u> ...' (Accuracy); 'You have to try to find out what things look like ...' (Shapes); 'I really do want you to ask yourself these questions and for the drawings to be the answers.' (Dowels)

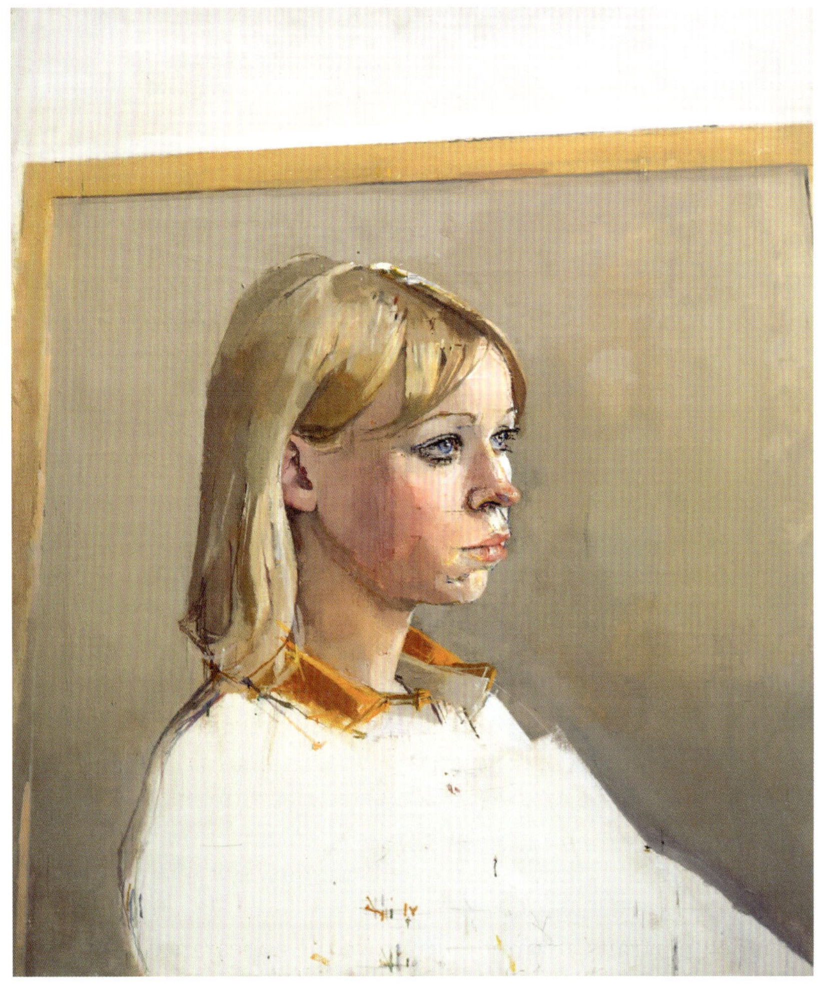

Janice Dilley 1967–9 · oil on canvas · 76 x 61 cm

A LETTER FROM PATRICK GEORGE

First published in the catalogue for 'A Singular Vision:
paintings of the figure by contemporary British artists',
Arts Council of England, 1985

DEAR NAOMI,

A letter is one thing an introduction something quite different. A letter is to somebody but how can I imagine who will read this and how can I write fairly about an exhibition when I am one of the artists taking part. It amounts to a description of a football match from one of the players.

The bunch of photocopies you sent me are all of paintings of people and they look to me as if they are of paintings made in the presence of the model. Unusual really, bearing in mind the practice in European painting over the last 800 years. The paintings are all of particular people, often with their names as the title. The way they look does not appear to have been made more pleasing by giving them smiles or longer necks (a tutor in one of the art schools I attended confided, 'you will never sell if you don't give them more neck'). I think I am right in saying that nearly all commissioned portraits attempt to improve the appearance of the sitter or at least overlook the socially undesirable features, the bags under the eyes, the red nose. The artist has been concerned for a long time with beauty and the ideal and how to improve upon the vagaries of the individual. Many of these paintings are of nudes, none of them seem Venuses, none appear to have been painted to appeal; if anything they are slightly off putting, their look standing across the stream of desire, reminding me only too clearly of prosaic awkward reality.

So what are these pictures about? They mostly seem about the unexpurgated appearance of people. Not realism which uses texture and the literary attributes but how a person looks, what reaches the artist through his eyes. To me appearance implies distance, something seen somewhere other than where you are yourself, usually beyond reach. From the appearance one can imagine the physical presence or some part of it (for a try at modelling reveals our amazing inadequacy in the appreciation of three dimensions).

If you paint a picture of a view through a window and are looking through the window panes and if after some time you open the window and see the view unimpeded by the glass you will experience a sharp surprise. I am writing this in a room which has a pair of windows overlooking the street. I have just opened one of the windows to test what I have written. The difference of the two views is obvious, perhaps more so because the windows are dirty. The closed window keeps me in my room and keeps the view the other side of glass. The grid of the glazing bars in my window lines up with or diverges from the rectangles of the windows across the road. The distances to the opposite wall with its windows and drain pipes are distances considered in relation to the surface of my window. The wall can be seen to run obliquely to my window but the wall of another house seems parallel. The scene is set back in order of depth something like the flats in a stage set. The sky can be seen like a bright rectangle, the brick walls as a darker fruit-cake type rectangle. The view is already in the two-dimensional terms of a canvas: all the houses, windows and sky are projections as a plane. The rectangle of infinite sky and rectangle of dense wall are in terms of art. The helicopter passing from left to right makes a track on the grass of a few degrees of inclination and could be a fly crawling rather quickly over the surface.

The other open window presents a great hole into which I could fall. There is a sense of vertigo and I feel at risk, the people across the road can see what I am doing. The street noises are louder, the walls are out there and I can get the scratchy feel of the bricks coming through my finger nails. The roofs are for cats to creep over. The space across the street to the opposite wall is like the space through a tunnel, I feel it is like that although I suppose it is exactly opposite to the light one sees at the end of a real tunnel, in fact, there, the eye travels across the light within the ditch of the street and meets up with the dark of the opaque

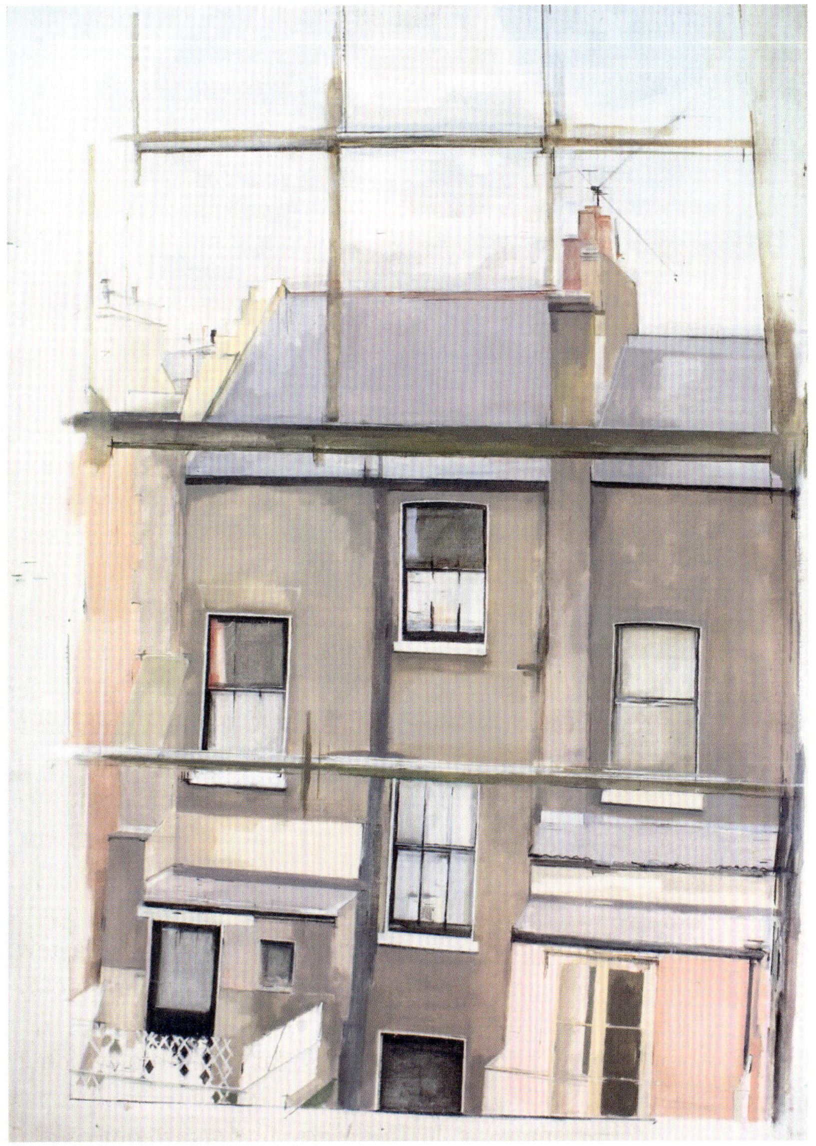

Moreton Terrace, Large View from the Back   1964–9 · oil on canvas · 152.4 x 106.7 cm

wall. The sky is the space above the roofs through which the aeroplanes fly. The helicopter that was coming towards me was probably flying above the winding river. The worry of the canvas is the worry of not falling out of the arena.

Some of the paintings deliberately distance the model. The models are visually examined, in others they are visually hugged. I do not suggest by this that the one attitude is more passionate than the other. The passion of Piero della Francesca, an artist of more than usual interest for some of these painters, is just as great as the obviously gushing passion of Rubens, and Rubens is another artist whom some of these painters have looked at closely.

Perhaps more than usual these artists have considered their work in relation to the work in the museums. Tracing their cultural ancestors would be exciting and unpredictable but is outside the scope of this letter.

The paint too has different roles. In some of the pictures the paint modifies the white canvas to suit the description. Like stone carving where the body can be imagined to be awaiting release from within the block, so the image can be imagined to lie inside the whiteness of the canvas and the colours by deducting from the all containing white can develop the canvas until the meaning is visible. The light falling on each patch of paint radiates the colour on its in and out journey through the film of paint (to the white priming and back).

The paint may be thicker, may blanket the ground, reflect mainly from its own surface: the heavier substance will show the brush stroke, and the direction and suggestion of energy given by the mark will contribute (with the ordering of the colour), to the description of the lie of the form: for example streaking across the floorboards, down the figures, around the nose.

When the paint is very thick the canvas becomes a mere support for the viscous substance. The paint now is obviously stuff, the density suggests the solid matter of the world we live in and the clearly channelled strokes show how the painter's arm was directed in response to his feel of the look. This corrugated surface attracts the forms of the eye so that despite the almost real gestures into space the surface is made clear.

Not that there is any illusion in any of the pictures in this exhibition. The paint is never made to simulate fur or metal or glass. The paint presents different kinds of description and the different descriptions give rise to the different look of the paintings.

To paint in the presence of a model is different. To be wide open to all that happens before your eyes as you sit there is special. I do not mean painting the name of the thing; nose, eyes, arms, legs – that seems to me a tradition backed by the authority of anatomy and perspective and has different aims. These were, I imagine the conventions Cézanne escaped, why Sickert said Cézanne's drawing was awful and why Cézanne's name was not welcome in The Slade of Tonk's time. The traditional rules of how things look tend to hide the view. What I mean now, is gaping at what is out there and then trying to account for it with paint on canvas, that's new. There are no longer any general rules unless it is that each picture must be unique. The artist makes his own rules usually borrowed from someone else and modified to suit his purpose; rules or procedures are necessary to get anything readable at all. Recent work on perception makes it clear that vision is partial, so there is no right vision and for a long time map makers have understood that the spherical world cannot be projected on a flat surface, in this case the canvas. The way is open and very complicated. The streams of messages from the subject are baffling and contradictory; changing all the time so that the artist cries out for some consistency, but despite the confusion knows that what is out there is it.

Here today and gone tomorrow; meanwhile there are two great subjects to describe while we are here: the place we find ourselves in and what the others look like. The exhibition is about the latter. Owing to the character of his art which is always now, the painter has the capacity more than most, to savour the present. Could there be a better way of passing the time than sitting in a field surrounded by the intense concentration of nature, or looking at a naked girl when the pose is right and the light even. We paint because it is all marvellous to look at, that's why.

Yours, Patrick

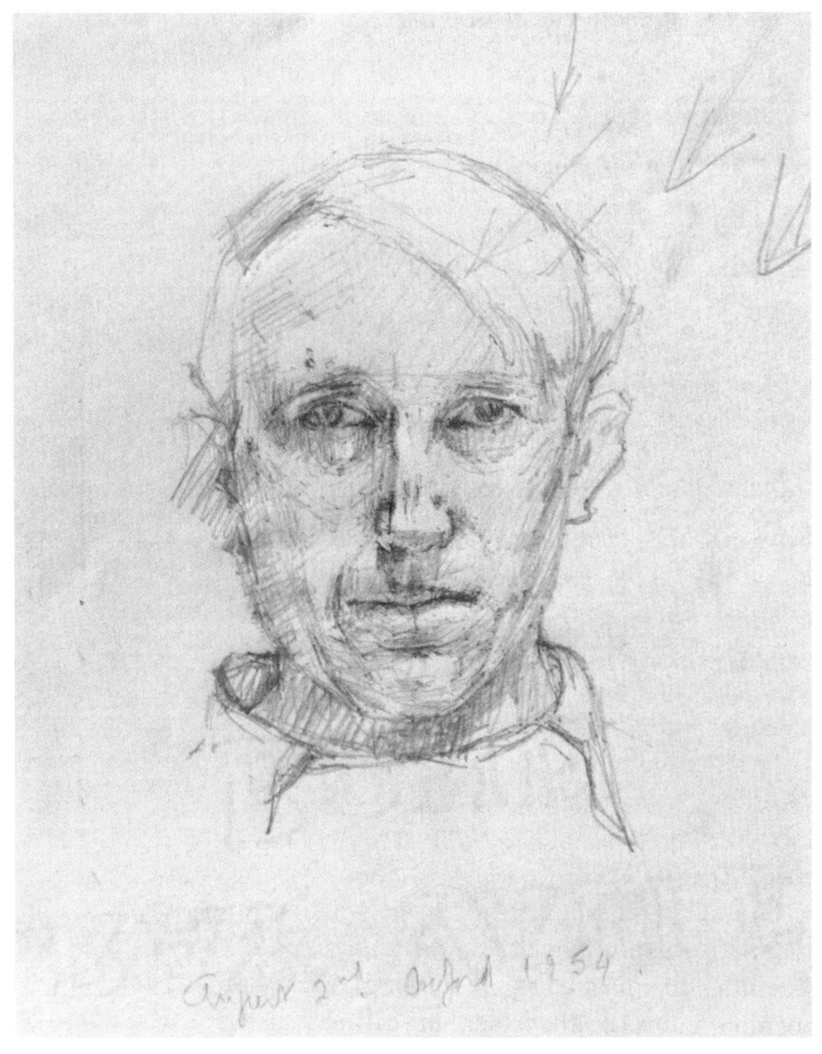

Self Portrait 1954 · pencil on paper · 18.4 x 13.3 cm

'INTRODUCTION'

First published in the catalogue for 'Drawings of
People: an exhibition of drawings selected for
the Arts Council by Patrick George', 1975

DRAWING TO ME MEANS THE MANAGEMENT OF ALMOST anything that can leave a mark. The lead comes out of the end of the pencil leaving a trail across the page; a boat is 'drawn' up the beach and leaves a furrow in the sand. The dictionary says the word derives from the Old English 'dragan' which suggests drag – the pencil is dragged across the page. Even the horse 'draws' the cart, which gives rise to a nice fanciful picture and also raises the question of whether it is not the driver by his management of the horse who is the draughtsman. The driver steers the horse and steering must be one of the most important ingredients in drawing. Other different uses of the word seem to have an un-expectedly close relationship to the artistic activity: for instance the marksman 'draws' a bead on his target which seems very like the drawing procedure of some artists. But mainly drawing is used to mean pulling and in the case of the artist the drawing is the trail left as evidence of the action.

Drawing is usually carried out with a pencil on a piece of paper. The paper is probably rectangular. The marks left by the pencil lie on this surface. If the mark is brief it may state only a position, a point on the paper here rather than there, near the edge or somewhere near the middle. If there is more than one mark the marks will relate to each other and set up suggestive patterns like the stars in their constellations. Or the marks may have con-tinuity and form lines and these will have length and lie in the direction of any of the 360° of the compass. The appreciation of the length and angle will depend to a great extent on their <u>com-parative relationship</u> and to the rectangle of the page. If the lines or marks fall very near each other they form a mass or area of tone. Tone modifies the brightness of the paper so the area covered by the tone differs from the uncovered area. The tone can be modulated, usually from light to dark so gradually taking the light from the paper. Tone is often referred to as shading and, as the word suggests, the shading casts a shade over the whiteness of the page. The use of marks showing position, lines having length and direction, and <u>tone</u> indicating a <u>change in surface</u> constitute the traditional language of drawing. However, these elements are often used for less easily defined functions; marks to indicate texture, lines wandering intermittently, and tone standing for local colour.

Most drawings possess this kind of geometry but more often than not also carry a description of appearance as it is the most convenient of visualising how things will work. Architects note down projections; doctors describe operations; yachtsmen the lines of their new boat; and I imagine Leonardo drew his inventions to see how they would work out. Some sculptors and painters use drawing as an auxiliary to their main work, both useful before starting or to get something clear when the work is in progress. This is distinct from those drawings which exist in their own right. In my experience these independent drawings are often carried out when the artist is going through a period of drawing rather than painting. Some artists, in the sense of using paper and pencil, do not draw at all.

Illustration is a form of description. When you draw something out of your head, for instance, if you try to draw a rabbit, you attempt to make marks that will add up to as recognisable an image as you can manage. There are specialists in drawing animals and boats, and numerous and attractive books on how to draw popular subjects. From these you learn a pattern for what you wish to indicate and then you modify the pattern to suit the particular occasion. A matchstick man can be made comparatively tall or short, an egg shape for a head can be made longer or more round. Illustration is how to make lines look like things and the success of the illustration depends upon the recognisability of the attributes of the subject. Most drawings of the past contain this ingredient.

Today if you want to keep an account of the appearance of what you are looking at why not take a photograph. The snapshot on the beach is an essential reminder of last year's holiday. Photographs identify people and places: surrounded by photographic images we accept them as how things look (however, when we take photographs for ourselves we reject some as too awful to be like). The photographic account seems to me as unusual as most and a squint through the viewfinder confirms this: the little scene is isolated, rosy, tame, already once removed and even more so after processing, when the printed picture will join all the rest of the family of glossy prints. I do not really understand why photographs always seem so nostalgic, why they remind me about how things 'used to be'. The instant the camera clicks the subject slips away into the past. Recently there was an exhibition of photographs called 'The Real Thing' but I feel more sympathy with an advertisement for Instamatic cameras that states 'memories are made of this'. <u>Reality, whatever that is, is in the present</u>. The artist attempting to draw what he sees, while he sees it, is always dealing with now, even though the drawing may take a long time. The drawing may even show a moment in time but unlike a photograph it rarely begs the question of which year. Van Gogh's people are wearing overcoats a hundred years out of date but we do not notice their old-fashioned clothes, rather we are reminded of the nature of the clothes we are wearing now.

Artists who draw what they are looking at are usually trying for a likeness. A likeness is difficult to define for it depends on an enormous variety of intentions and also on what the artist allows himself to see. One of the many reasons for this prejudiced view is that the artist comes to his subject with a requirement. He may want to draw a head before he has decided on any particular head, so it seems likely that he has some notion of what he hopes to find before he starts. The likeness he wishes to make may not be a recognisable image but an abstraction of lines suggested by what he is looking at. The likeness will then depend on his ability to record these lines. Despite this prejudice, in the course of trying to do this, a particular description of an object may arrive on his paper. In any case the artist's idea of the likeness will almost certainly change as he examines his subject and considers it in the light of what is appearing on his paper. <u>So in a way he does not know what he is drawing until he has drawn it</u>.

When any of us look at an object we look at it from where we are, and where the object is, is somewhere else. <u>We see the object because its appearance reaches us</u>. Epicurus describes objects as giving off skins or films of appearance. Thinking this way we can imagine all the visible world radiating these films (perhaps like the shimmering waves of heat that rise from a hot road). In every direction the objects give off their skins of appearance and our glance catches the set appropriate to where we are. To reach us the appearance must be uninterrupted and continuous all the way back along the field of view and into the eye. If we were to cut the line of appearance anywhere we would find the image intact; just as we find the writing running all through a stick of rock (in this case it would be more like if the stick were conical). The magic is that the appearance arrives from different distances but when we see them they are all the same distance from us, at the back of our eye. Our eyes scan the view, the images press into our eyes and from them we interpret a coherent pattern of appearance. Images of the nearer objects overlap at the edges as our two eyes receive their particular view. This varying vibration of images seems an essential part of our experience of looking and one that the camera automatically extinguishes. The appearance that reaches us from the object is only the most superficial aspect of that object, the outermost surface of what we see (the powder and rouge of the face). Like touch, for we only touch the lipstick yet experience the nature of the head, so with our sight we may seem to touch what we are looking at.

The artist with his pencil and paper tries to account for this bewildering state of appearance. His own passion for what he is looking at leads him like any lover into a distortion of the facts. He loves the appearance which is why I suppose Constable said 'I never saw an ugly thing in my life but let the form of an object be what it may, light shade and perspective will always make it beautiful'. The view comes to him but to him it seems out there where the object is. Frequently the artist mistakes this appearance for reality, falls in love with his model but fails to recognise her in the street. The artist, drawing what he is looking at, is paying tribute to this beauty of appearance so at times he may believe that the doing of the drawing is more important than the result. Poking the pencil at the image of a person is not a passive action but is like going around the person themselves. The artist is catching a likeness and making off with one of their skins of appearance. It is no wonder, the activity has always aroused suspicion: the power to draw regarded as a special gift and the drawing as evidence of magic.

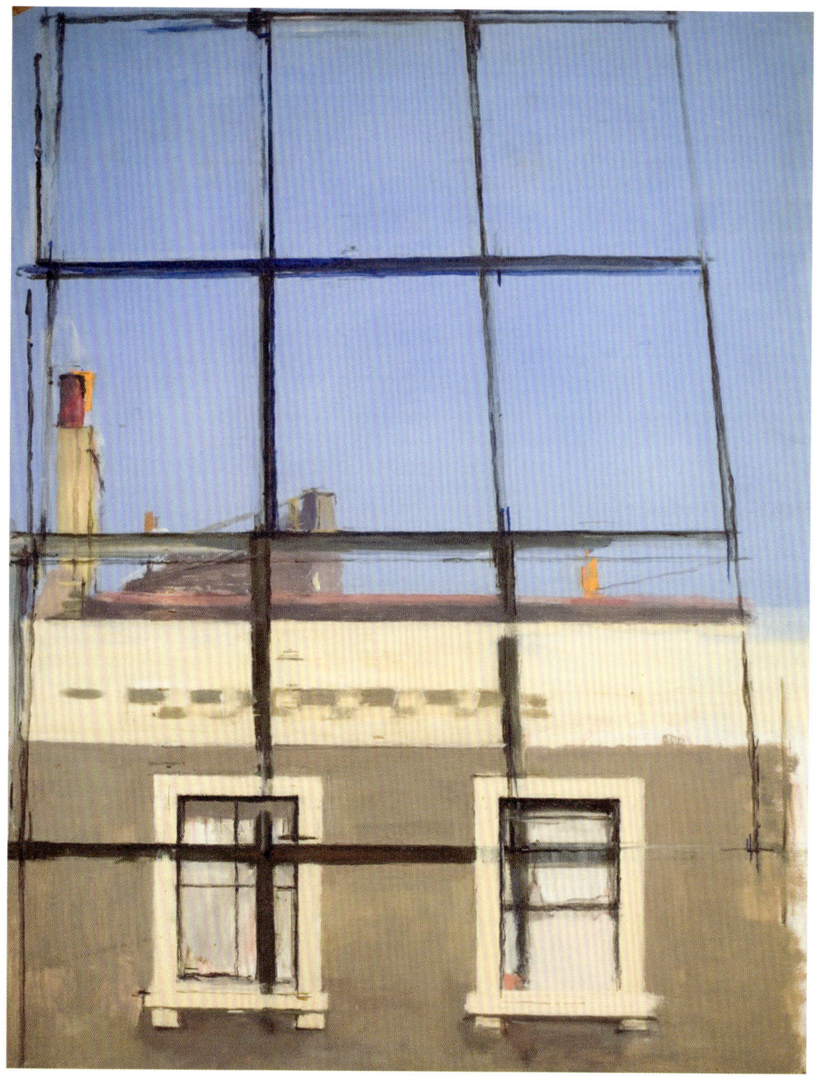

Blue Sky in Pimlico   early 1980s · oil on wood · 61 x 45.7 cm

PAINTING WHAT
YOU CAN SEE FROM
A SINGLE VIEWPOINT

First published in *Uppercase,* issue no. 4, 1960

IF YOU LIKE WHAT YOU SEE THEN IT SEEMS NATURAL TO try and describe the thing you like. Painting is an expedient way of doing this.

But why from a single viewpoint? When I notice something I stop to look at it. It has always seemed to me that my way of looking corresponds to a series of single views, and I do not think they are views seen in the round – my visual experience does not correspond to the experience of free standing sculpture, when there is more round the other side than I expected. I believe I see in views of high relief, for instance the angle between the pavements and the houses is opened out more than 90°.

Also because it is the particular relationships from a single view that are interesting. It is usually from just somewhere that I am struck by what I see and nowhere else will do or be the same. At once my position becomes significant, and the longer I stay there the more important my position becomes. The subject holds me fast by radiant lines to my eye like guy ropes to a tent pole.

One more reason is that it is the only way I have found of making a representation of what I can see and so being able to catch some indisputable facts that do not simply depend on my own opinions.

It is not easy to see. The partiality of vision is well known. The selection of what is useful to see for everyday life varies with each person. Some people hardly look at all. They use a code of recognition similar to the abbreviations of recognition used by the army – 'all trees are fir trees or bushy topped'. Everyone has their sight conditioned by every experience, not by any means just visual experience. We are all prejudiced and very conservative in what we recognise from what we see. It would anyway be impossible to get through everyday life if we looked at everything. Few people are interested in looking at the actual appearance of things and few painters are interested in the problem of painting what they see in front of them. Painters look at pictures, their own, fine art, coarse art, photographs, advertisements, everything, so what they choose to see is not only conditioned by their everyday rationalisation, but includes their own aesthetic preference; it is likely that they only choose to paint what is paintable and what echoes their experience of pictures.

But if it is not easy to see it is certainly more difficult to translate what you see into two dimensions even from a single viewpoint. By this I do not mean a fixed stare, but using the amount of scansion necessary to view the subject.

The picture starts off uniquely. Each seems brand new and different from any other and the painter has high hopes and an arrogant assurance of success. The paint looks beautiful on the clean canvas and the subject looks innocent. One hopes to ride in like a surf bather on a wave of enthusiasm, but the doubts come, are ignored, yet persist. The subject changes, wriggles clear and inviolate and the canvas looks like paint. The picture comes to a stop, the subject still looks beautiful, perhaps in a different way, and the canvas looks like yet another of one's pictures – it is a moment of despair, when one understands the absolute difference between the canvas, the horrible canvas and the beautiful thing one sees. One has lost, so one casts about for anything, anything that will establish a connection between the canvas and the thing one looks at.

I think it is possible to establish some sort of elementary comparative similarity between the canvas and the appearance of the subject. Looking at a window it may be possible to tell whether it appears higher than it is long and it is possible to mark off on the canvas two distances with this comparative similarity. So one builds up a system of empirical proportions – the distances and intervals alike and unlike, the same, greater or less. Each time one finds a new 'position' and its corresponding ratio with what has gone before, so one more comparative fact has been gathered from the subject and each is precious, particularly the ones of absolute certainty – slowly the picture accumulates information,

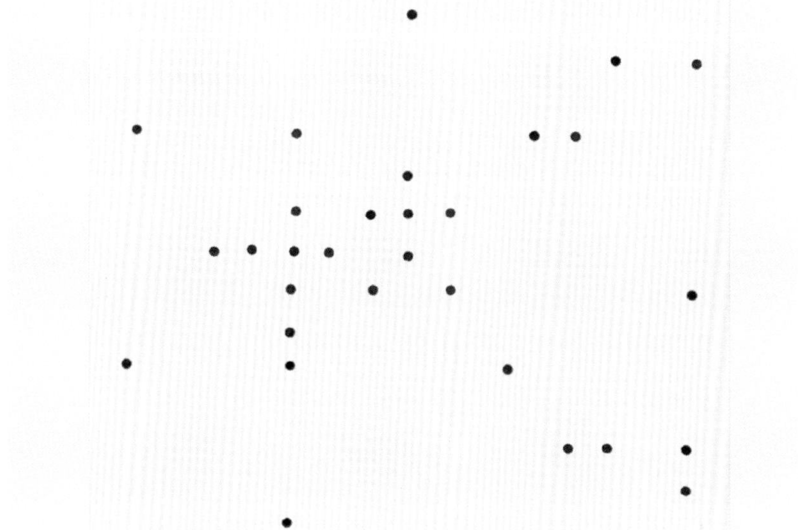

Object. Paper spots arranged in considered positions.

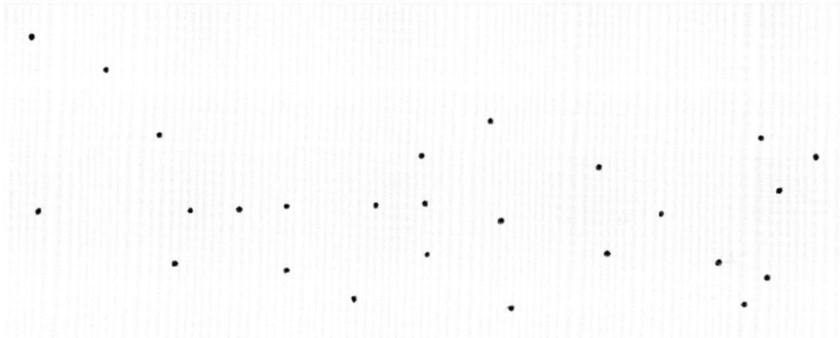

Drawings of positions from a similar object.

the like distances and intervals make a rhythm which multiplies across the canvas. The first distances become significant units and their length (in fact the first distance) is the measure of every other position. The subject is still as completely beautiful, the canvas remains like a ledger; the marks of interval describe what has been found out. They are selective, but in so far as the answers are correct they are outside the influence of opinion.

A number of positions can be described by a line. The object can be seen in terms of a collection of reciprocal lengths. The

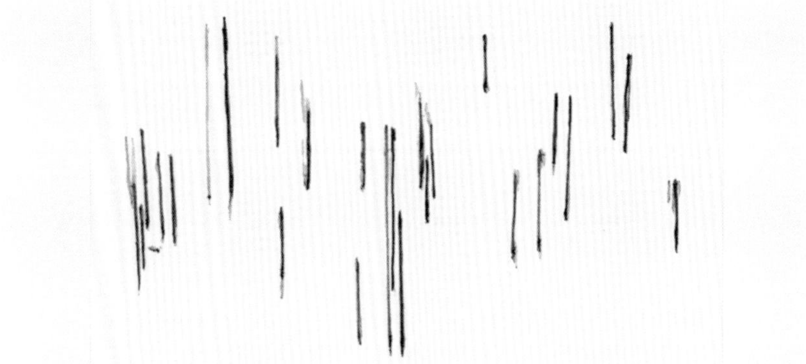

Drawing. Objects whose apparent length is affected by the distance away from the eye.

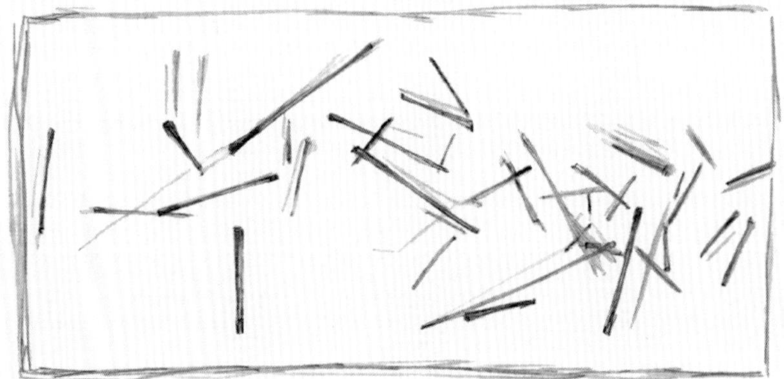

Drawing. Objects whose apparent length is affected by the angle to the eye.

lengths smaller or longer depending on the proportions of the object, the distance away, and the angle they make to the eye. (It is not easy to see the receding railway track as a near vertical line.) The first line on the canvas is qualified by the second and so is understood to be longer, shorter or the same, and the lines of apparently the same length echo each other. The lines have direction; they point in the same or different ways implying movement that is halted or reinforced; they lie on the canvas and their tilt and balance make an equilibrium with the rectangle. They may join end to end to become an articulated line whose length is made from the sum of the parts, they grow like a shoot into twigs and all the articulations are like the branches of one tree. Seen

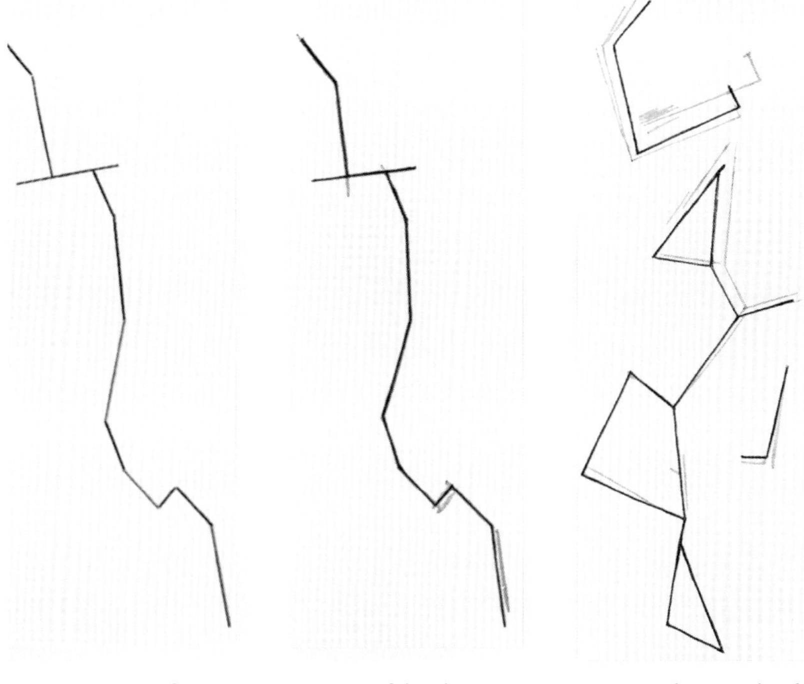

Object. Straws to form
a sequence of related
lengths.

Drawing of the object.
The lengths make an
articulated line – a
character.

Drawing. The articulated
line lengths makes
enclosures.

simultaneously the articulated line becomes a character. The appearance of the object is translated into these characters. The characters whose shapes depend on the view-point (because they do not exist in the actual object) can, if made without mistake, lead to an unprejudiced account.

If the articulated line joins on itself it cuts off an area of the canvas. The area is described by the lines like a field surrounded by hedges; the limits of a field may be described by hedges, but the field is not the sum of the hedges and the shape is not the sum of the lines. These shapes particular to your point of view have to be identified as two-dimensional patterns so that they may be made on the canvas. A rectangular tabletop cornerwise on becomes a diamond shape. When things are placed on the table the top is obscured and new shapes are made. If the objects overlap they lose their familiar outline: the side of a matchbox

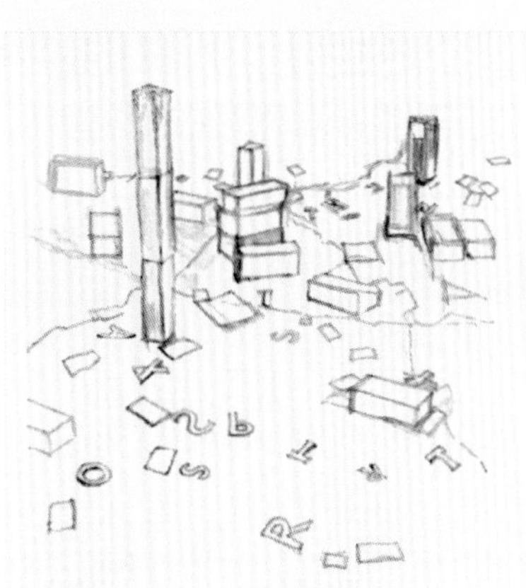

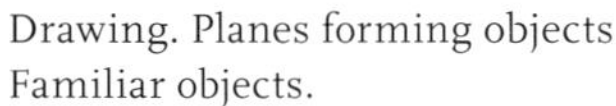

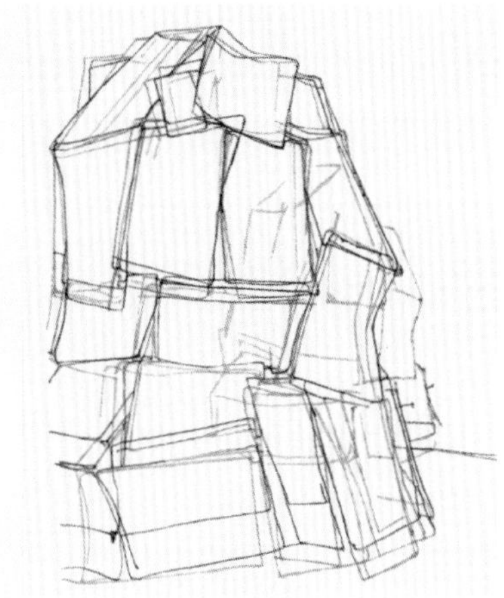

Drawing. Planes forming objects. Familiar objects.

Drawing. The surfaces are drawn again and again until they form one object.

becomes a yellow flag, a piece of table a cooling tower, the arrises of the inkwell cranes and signal arms, the half-seen dish a moon.

The shapes are juxtaposed into an irregular mosaic. The adjacent shapes condition each other by their common boundaries until they lock together and form a third shape that encloses them both and is more than the sum of the two. The shapes expand, each continually refined to accommodate the last, and the last by a series of compound comparisons influences the appearance of the first. The shapes expand until they add up to a description of the diamond-shaped tabletop. Some shapes are more difficult to see than others – if the real-life shape is in elevation then it is easier to translate than if it is seen obliquely, like the tabletop or a field. It is the oblique shape, the surface running away from the eye that is the difficulty. It is incompatible with the surface of the canvas. In the translation one's mind has to force the far boundaries forward and the near surfaces back so that they can be comprehended in terms of their optical appearance. Malevich's picture of a single yellow plane receding into infinity seems to me a marvellous illustration of this crisis of appearance. I believe everyone is aware of this when they stand looking over the sea. The impossibility of mentally tipping into elevation what we know to be a huge flat area stimulates our appreciation of what a great

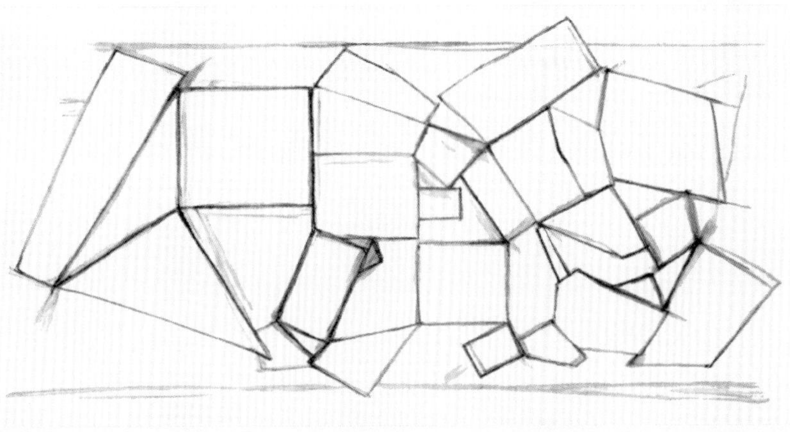

Drawing. Juxtaposed shapes. Precision makes them fit.

distance we are looking over. We are never more aware of how far we can see away from us than in the absolutely flat parts of East Anglia; mountains which are landscapes in elevation, do not so particularly stimulate our sense of distance. The single viewpoint painter has to make the difficult imaginative effort to see the horizon and foreground in the same plane, the plane the shapes occupy on the canvas.

This particular recognition of the two-dimensional appearance constitutes an appreciation of the three-dimensional form; far from projecting himself into the three dimensions of the object, which is a way of reducing the appearance to what we expect to find, this effort to see flat the three-dimensional object provokes the sense of form by describing the difference found between the real-life object and the canvas. These ways of coming to terms with the thing in front of us depend on relative proportions. (With certain reservations these proportions can be gauged with the help of a brush or pencil held at arm's length and at right angles to the line of sight.) The time is spent exactly co-ordinating the proportionate lengths and intervals and directions. The marks are made again and again until the pattern rings true, or as true as the painter can make it, the actual look of the picture is det-ermined by when the painter leaves off, and often he does so

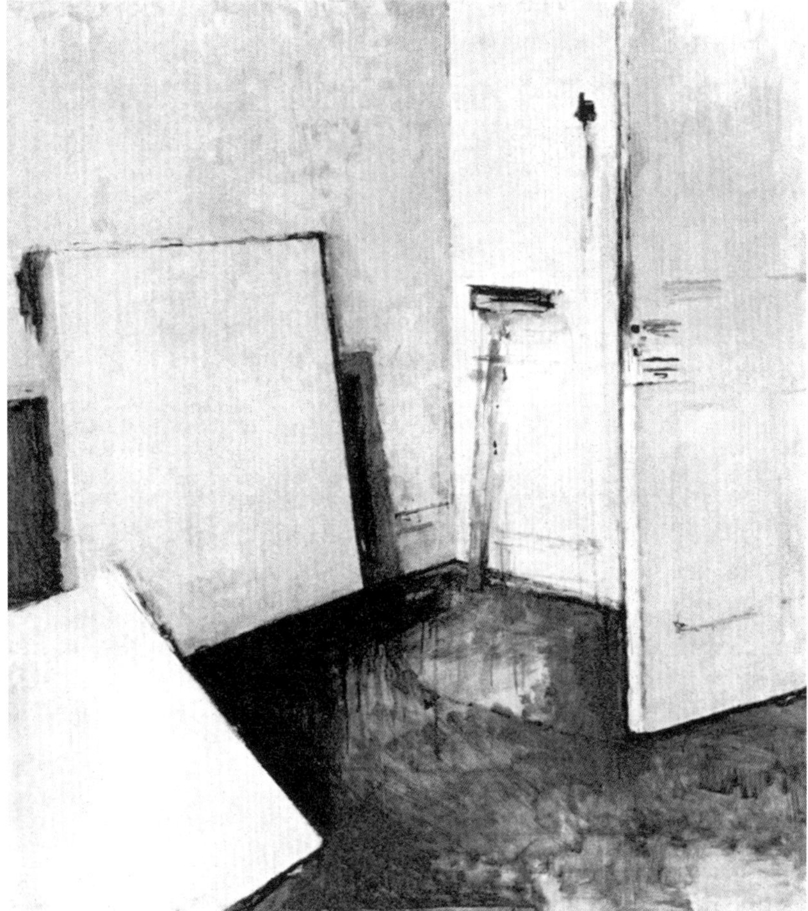

... the appearance of the subject always changes and there is no absolute solution

for quite circumstantial reasons: the leaves fall off the tree, the model cannot come any more. But the amount of content that he manages to correlate mainly depends on his own capacity; obviously great painters can manage more than less great. The picture at first seems to go swiftly, but as more information is gathered and brought to bear on what has gone before the pace slackens like a graph that first rises steeply, but as time passes eases off until the curve flattens out and hardly advanced against the time spent. The changes get smaller but are as difficult to make. Like the tide coming in, the waves go back and forth and it is often necessary to spoil what is done before the painter can get further. Sometimes the wave goes out and does not come back, but in any case the picture will never be finished. The knowledge and selection from the appearance of the subject always changes and there is no absolute solution. The picture does not stand for a reflection of the object but for a prejudiced account – for the visible compound of experiences and the efforts to translate them in front of the object.

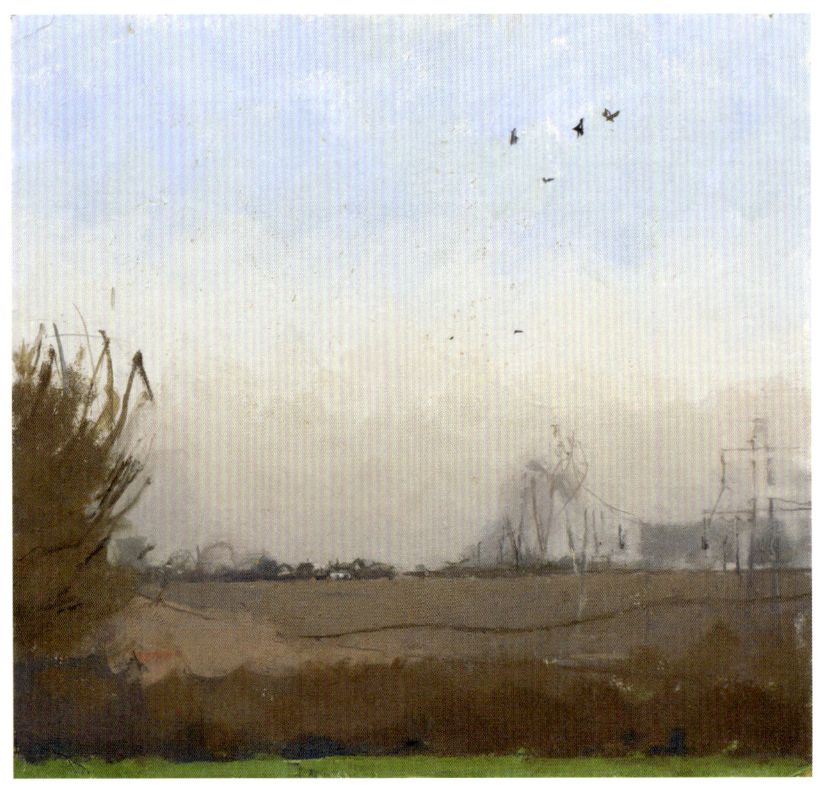

Winter Landscape, Hickbush   1960 · oil on board · 38 x 38 cm

NOTES ON PAINTING

Extracts from the personal diary of Patrick George 1967–78

AS THE LIGHT SLOWLY LIFTS AND THE FOG BRIGHTENS and the birds twitter more, then the lightness lifts the top of one's head. Things seem clearer, something infectious from the hidden sun stirs me up to happiness.

I think one first flounders around waiting for a brush stroke to stick. Sitting there watching the spring bowling past. If you imagined the pylons as Nelson's ships in line then you might fancy them somewhat differently from what they are.

What do we mean when we think 'I can't paint it.'

The crops are the clothing of landscape. I want the paint mark so LIKE as to convince – the paint mark has the authority of the moment. Do not forget this subject hardly existed – except in earlier spring. That now about to start I am undecided. Looking for something which is hard to recognise.

Sometimes it's like that, with the tide slowly going out of the picture. The spark ebbing away – imperceptibly weakening day by day – even as the effort is increased.

Whatever one may say about existentialism I should like to paint the grand landscape. The last great painters of the grand landscape were Claude and Rubens, Constable tried, Crome tried, Koninck.

Artists are not interested in what they are painting, they are moved by it. The art schools and their projects interests the students – no students expect to find art interesting. Art is not like that.

Though probably not advisable nor productive, I like matching nature stroke for stroke.

Winter Landscape, Hickbush　　　　late 1970s · oil on board · 40 x 55.9 cm

I am a second class artist with first class dreams.

·

By proportional measurements I try and assuage my despair.

·

All there is to landscape is the book lying open at the text. The more passionately they are appreciated the harder it is to draw a line in the correct geometrical direction.

·

You are the rhythm of the field – expressed by the hedgerow. You put on a rhythmic gesture to correspond. Eventually an elongated diamond shape – non rhythmic – with no flow emerges from the repeated efforts to see its evident rhythm. So perhaps it could have been better not to feel it in the first place – the first place feel is the driving force that keeps you at it, but apparently no more.

·

I am always suspicious of glorious days. This showed its true colours with a blinding rain storm after then, racy picturesque clouds and blue sky. The wind pouring over the trees and nature determined to make clear that she would not be measured. There is nothing to do on days except regard the guttering.

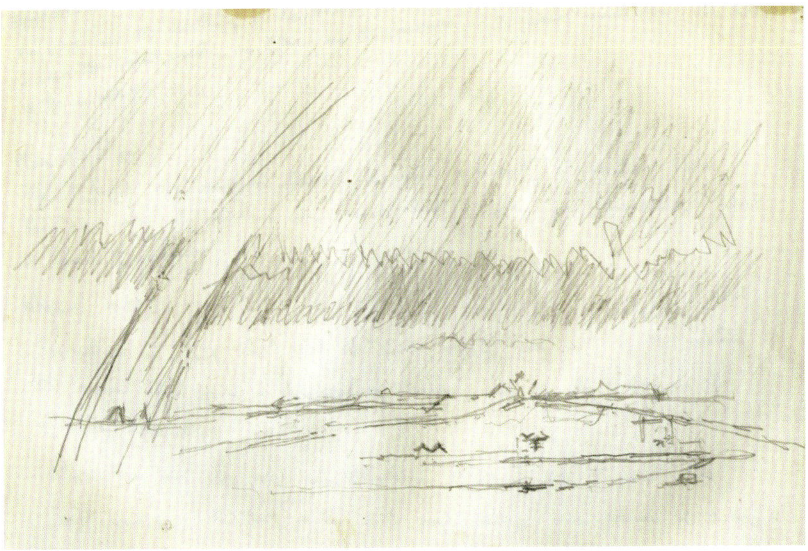

Diary sketch

There are times, many times, when there is no contact between the picture on the canvas and the scene to be painted – there seems to be no connection. Then the observation of proportions correspond to the ratios in the painting [and] can re-establish the contact.

.

Sketching is making gestures towards description. Description takes a long time. The unpremeditated eventually turns out to be the only interesting bit but one must have a plan.

.

The whole business is chance and to a great extent circumstantial. The view changes for better or worse – make no mistake, the view always changes.

.

Changes that have taken place in Delmars Field landscape:
Hay field; Hay cut; Rake and turned; Burnt; Gate closed; Horses moved; Cows and horses enter two fields; Barley green; Ripens; Grows, changes hedge line; Laid; Cut lower line; Baled lower line again; Grazed field turns silver, edges eaten clean; Hedge grows, flowers change; Hedge line falls lower; Stacks of barley bales hide

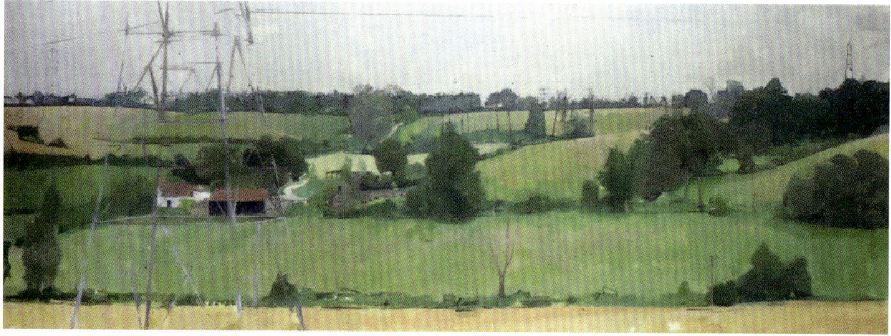

The Opposite Bank aka ***Delmers Farm***   1983 · oil on canvas · 83.8 x 213.3 cm

the view; It is days and evenings like this that tempt; To resist is difficult.

·

Rubens and Claude seem the only painters of grand landscape. Why did Cézanne choose not to paint 'Poussin' type landscapes. What's painting – transposition?

·

There is measuring and measuring. It's the actual … I am alive to look at the view.

·

This is an art of chance. The wind knocking the trees about, the measurements either more or less, there is no certainty and to make matters worse, the light is just right.

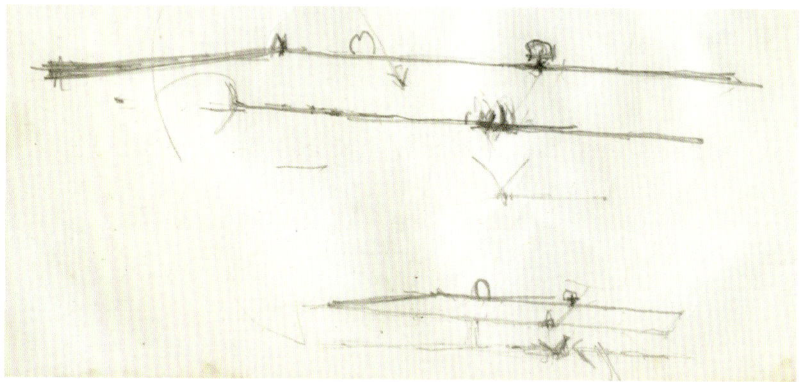

Diary sketch

What an afternoon – pale blue-bleached grass – shining yellow fields, grey trees, white clouds. Luminous. What to do about it – paint it. There are things one cannot just let pass – I mean things seen, moments of the day.

.

I think the assumption by most people that there is such a thing as a straight picture that is such a bore. Just as at that assumption one understands the speaker to be a non-starter.

.

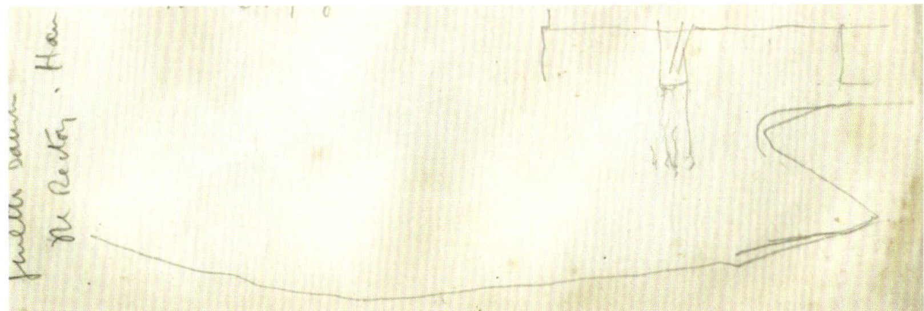

Wish to draw the sea. Find the sea. The view of the sea which reflects the idea. Who knows why they draw anything – often because the subject suggests a drawing. A subject is the abstract of lines which interest as well as being an interesting subject. This is the starter and the tempter and it also reflects what the artist has been looking for. As opposed to illustration, a found likeness. Lines suggested rather than subject suggested.

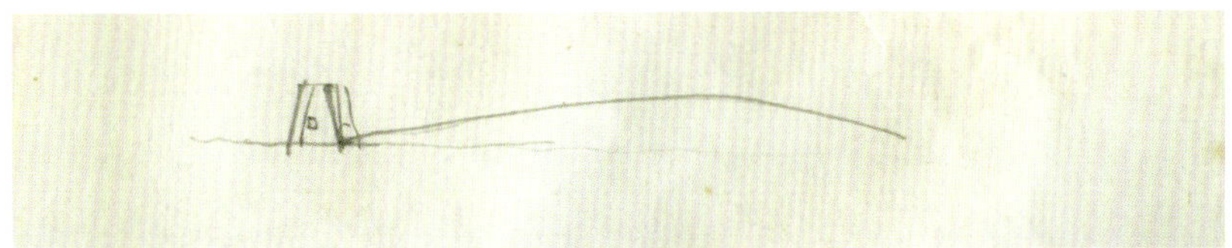

.

Some subjects lend themselves to drawing, like masts of boats.

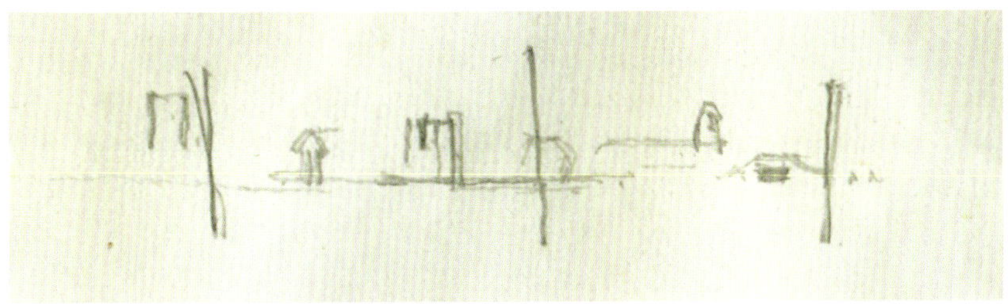

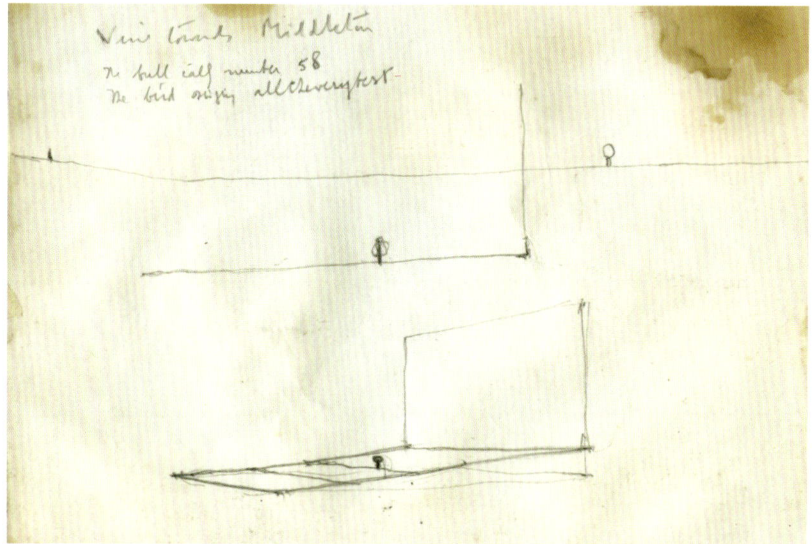

Diary sketch

When you look at a roof it seems tempting to go around it with a pencil. It will depend upon his ability to record the lines. They may eventually suggest a landscape. The subject may eventually be represented but almost despite the artist's attention to the name of the subject he is looking at. To what the object is called. Of course the subject may arrive on the page or it may be that the subject which claims his attention is some satisfactory abstraction of lines suggested by what he sees. The likeness will then depend on his ability to record their lines. In the course of trying to do this, despite his inattention, [the] description of an object may arrive on his paper. In any case the artist [who] draws what he is looking at finds that this idea about what he is looking at changes. He finds out how it looks, what it looks like, and this almost certainly will not be what he appreciated at first. So in a way he does not know what he is drawing until he has drawn it.

.

One's fancy is always running away inventing romances into the buildings and the trees – the measurement keeps some rein on these indulgences and pulls one back to what may be there and what may not be there.

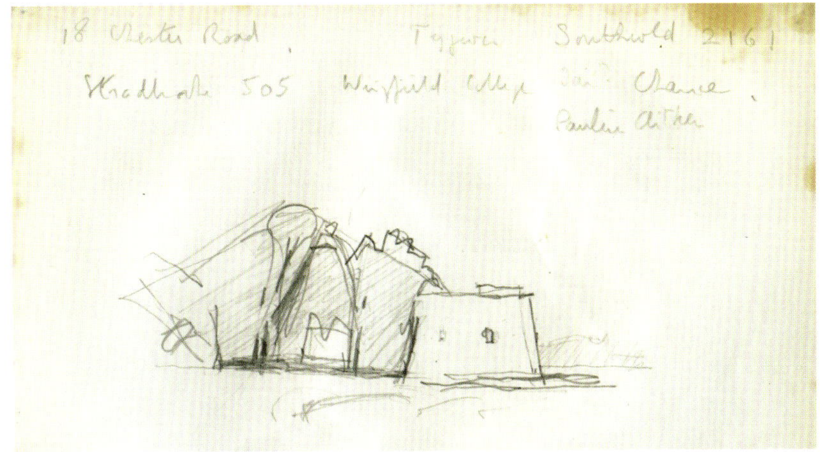

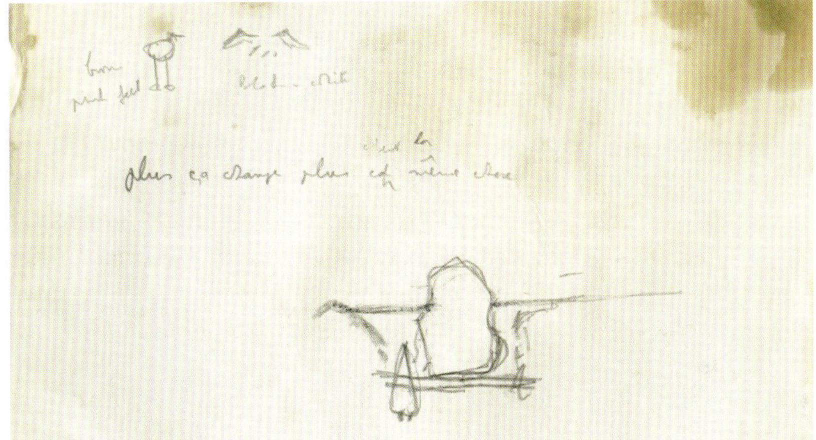

Diary sketches

It is a windy, sunshiny spring afternoon. The wind blows my measuring arm so that I can't believe in the observations. The wind by its buffeting annoys. The sun too, casting quaint shadows across the barn seems only worthwhile because it keeps me warm. At this moment Easter Monday changes have occurred in the appearance of the subject since I started: the green lorry was moved sometime in the winter, the foreground was fawn for stubble, brown for plough and is now green, the growth changes the contour. The background fields are now exactly recovered in colour, the brownish over green and the green over brown.

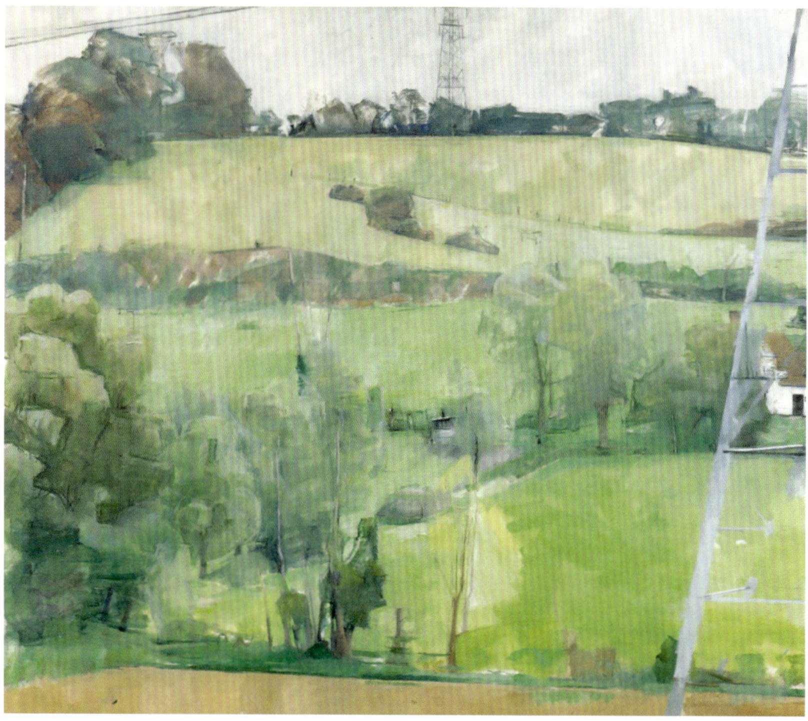

Valley Farm

1982 · oil on canvas · 101.5 x 112 cm
© Crown Copyright, UK Government Art Collection

The trees of course lost their leaves and now are growing them again (a surprisingly unimportant aspect). The window of the pig houses have been taken away and are mostly covered by sacks. The manure heaps have been taken away and are now back. The bales of straw in the two Dutch barns have now been demolished so that I can see right through under the roofs of both barns. The parked tractors and implements come and go. The background disappears on misty days, or like today is very clear. A small tree was felled behind the machinery shed. The corrugated iron barrier has been replaced by a gate.

·

A personal anthology by Jorge Luis Borges. He was disturbed by the fact that a dog at 3:14 (seen in profile) should have the same name as the dog at 3:15 (seen from the front). His own face in the mirror, his own hands surprised him on every occasion.

Berkley quote: 'Some truths there are so near and obvious to the mind that a man need only open his eyes to see them.'

·

Perhaps he meant that the physical world is implicit in its entirety in each manifestation just as in the same way, will, according to Schopenhauer, is implicit, in its entirety, in each individual.

·

He framed the view in the theatre because it prevents the spectators from forgetting unreality (which is the necessary condition of art).

·

Bad art is an art that makes false reports. Bad art is inaccurate art.

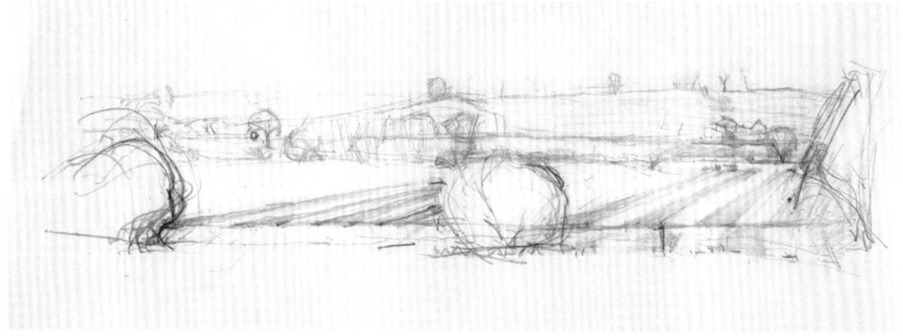

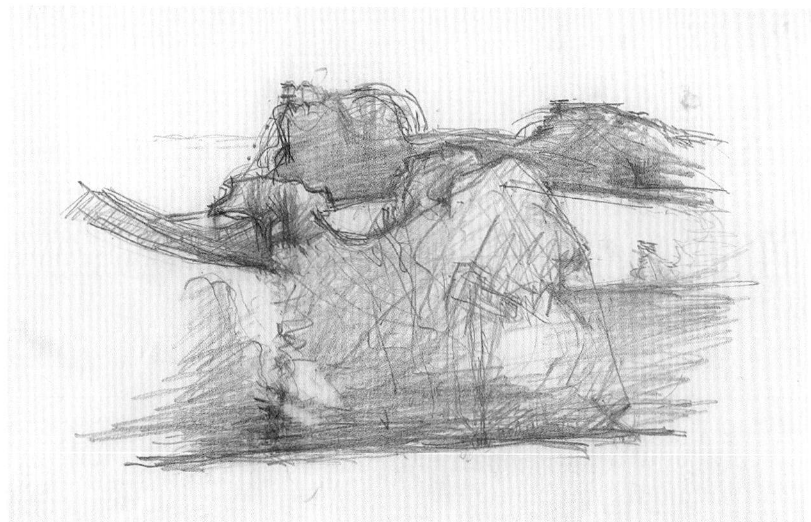

Hickbush sketches, 1960s

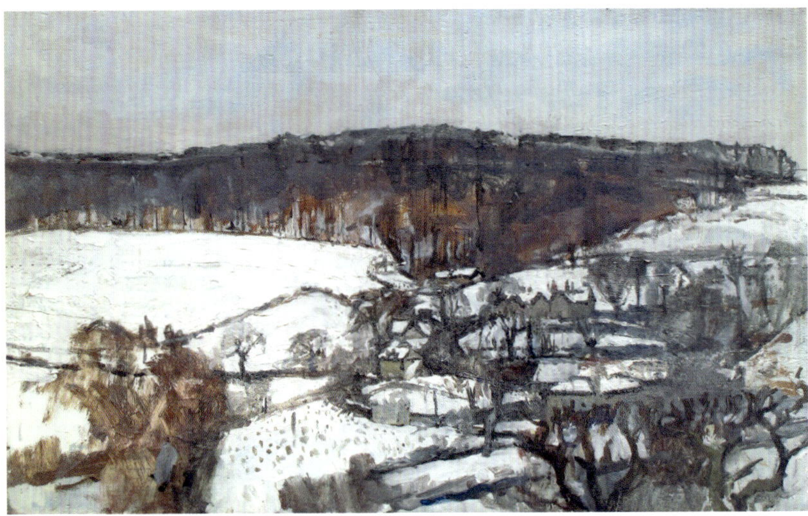

Sheepscombe in the Snow   *c.*1948 · oil on panel · 40.6 x 62.9 cm

One justification for winter painting is that amidst the snows and fogs you do get a touch of stability. But this is not the real reason for sitting out there in the wet and cold, it is its sheer particular beauty that matters. Its appearance, and how the thing is said to look, are different.

·

The activity seems more appropriate because one cannot be identified as an amateur sketcher nor does one feel like a sightseer. In winter the facts gathered despite the weather (the wind and cold) seem more precious. Perhaps the attraction is that one is stealing appearances against the odds so that anything one can put down has a precious value, almost anything. In the numbing cold of the north wind with fingers aching and clumsy and a face [set] hard [on] the windward side and toes [ringing] with the cold, any paint stroke adhered to the canvas (and some do not) seem a triumph. In some way it seems a greater privilege to view the frosty red, yellow-green, frosty sky and the brilliant moon than all the lush summer greens. Maybe one is less familiar with the winter view, the yellow sky: the lighting changes from fog with its pastel shades to the clearness of the crystal blue frosty weather, the Dutch seem the only painters to have tried it including Breughel.

You can't change all the picture all the time. The proportions won't change, nor more or less will some of the shapes. But the colours will change and even their relationship to the other colours will change. The colour, the skin of coloured paint on the canvas does not want to be emasculated or schematic or diagramatic. It wants to be as 'now', as the disposition. The drawing of the colour wants to be as present as the drawing of the limit. The limits can be searched for; in a way that seems impossible. (Outside with the changing light.) For the middles – the area – the surface, answering back. So the middle seems more muddled than the edges and the edges have the attention. Yet the simple beauty of the view is all shape with middle and edge equal, unemphatic and plain.

.

Try to get rid of the hard shrill viridian. Fussy.

.

Painting the seemingly dark trees against the sky [I] remember that for some reason that I do not understand why they have to be painted much paler than they seem to look.

.

If you just want information for a picture then it does not matter much what the weather is like or how the crops are changed. You just go to collect what you want like shopping and ask at the counter for so much of this and half a yard of that. But there are reasons for returning to the motif. For testing the idea. For

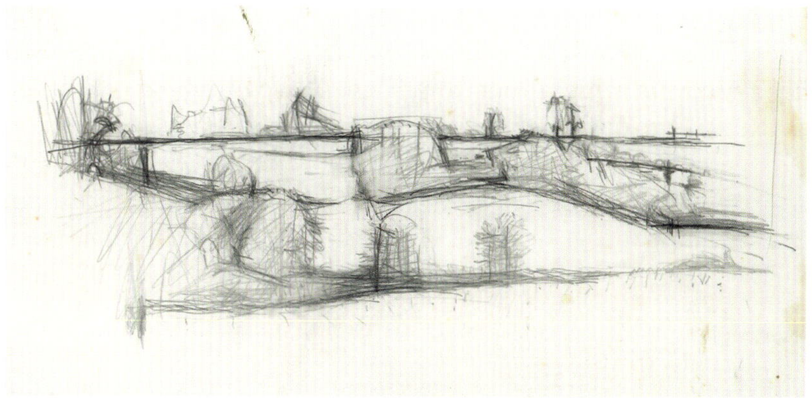

Hickbush sketch, 1960s

questioning how or where the idea slipped away from you the previous day. For trying again to unlock the essence from the scene. For then one needs the scene, and as originally found and loved. You stand there waiting, hoping you will catch a glimpse, a remembrance and all the while the tractor motors to and fro leaving behind new chocolate coloured stripes. And totally the season moves on.

.

That slip of the wrist that those old pros had for making good their demonstration life drawings on the student's paper was, it seemed, magic, but in retrospect seems convention. The bit that did not carry out their instructions but went in for proprieties sake. This was the bit that Cézanne either could not or would not manage and is why he was said not to be able to draw. This is the

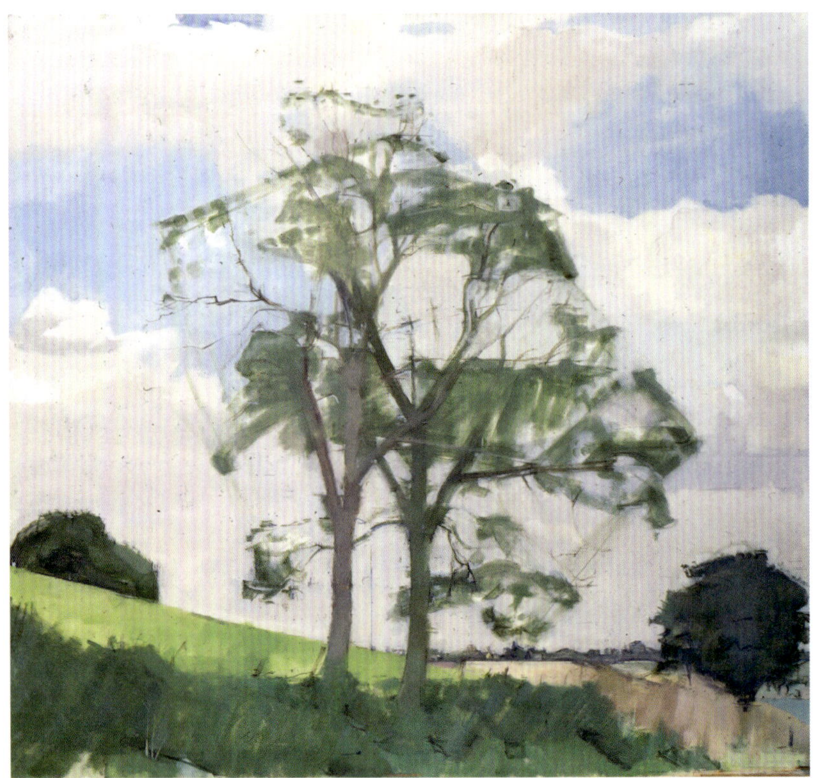

Two Ash Trees, Hickbush   c.1980s · oil on canvas · 101.6 x 106.8 cm

Empty Landscape   1967–8 · oil on canvas · 140 x 95 cm

bit that it is incredibly hard to keep out for it shields loss of face and ineptitude. I take it that this is one reason for Coldstream's procedure.

.

The circumstantial changes and difficulties particular to painting a landscape outside:

Shadow on the canvas.

The weather: blue mostly or clear or dark; clouds or no clouds; the sun moving around during the day; the wind blowing the canvas, changing direction so that what once bellied out now caves in; the rain wetting the palette; rain before you begin (it is difficult to set out in the rain); cold chills the fingers, brain and feet; dazzling sunlight on the canvas; the wind buffeting the measuring arm making it eventually impossible to measure – impossible to dangle a plumb line; the wind blowing the leaves silver side up and bending the trees into different positions; rain turning the grass green and the earth dark.

Insects getting in your clothes and flying around, settling on canvas.

The farming operations: the fields ripening and then cut, plowed, dunged, harrowed, burnt so the field changes from pale

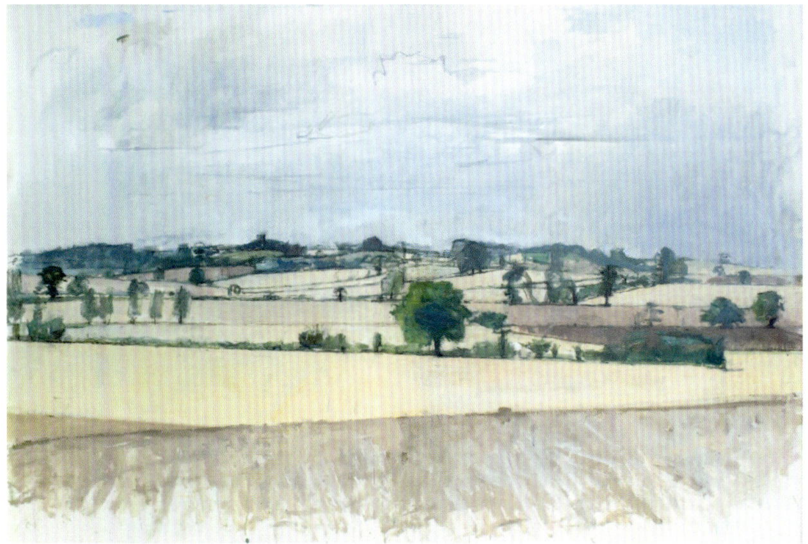

Hickbush Extensive Landscape from the Oaks   1961 · oil on canvas · 101.6 x 152.4 cm

ochre to navy blue; the smoke obscuring the view; the smell of pig manure – not a bad hazard; the mosquitos; the spectators, including the farmer and labourers – gardeners.

Getting the canvas to the site and the paints; all the porteridge necessary; the rigging of the easel, spades, hammers, planks.

The suitable clothes – warm shoes, boots, somewhat weather-proof jacket; performing in time to the weather.

The distraction of the rats.

·

The success or failure of a landscape painting depends to a great part on the succession of the weather. There is nothing like fog for finishing you off.

·

In parts for different days.

·

Do outwardly what we do surreptitiously. Is not this what all discoveries of new likeness have done. A question of facing the facts.

·

You do not admire the subject in Matisse? Not often. That is to say you are not directed to admire the subject as in Claude Lorrain.

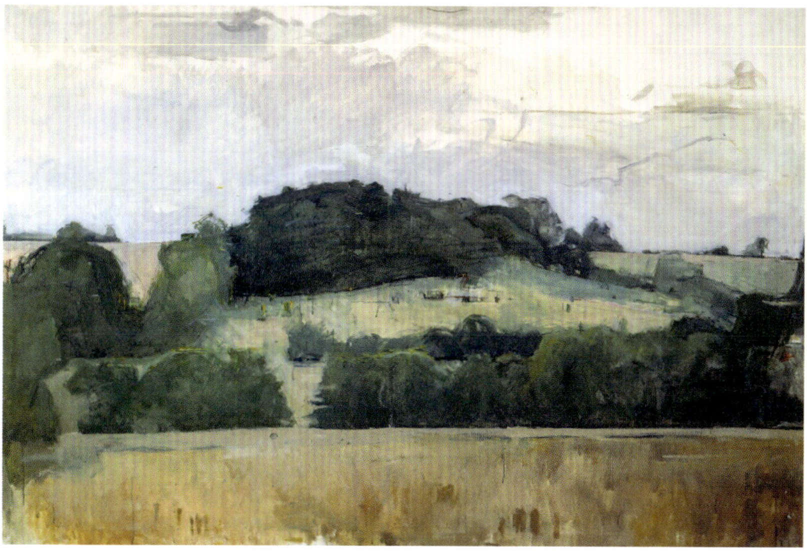

Hickbush　　　　　　　　1961 · oil on board · 101.6 x 152.4 cm

What I admire in a picture:

Reason, order, following another man's reasoning.

The clarity, the explicitness of what he has to say and his affection, which may come in the explicitness.

Internalisation. 'Likeness' to me is like a deep conversation, actively listening to the artist's surroundings which further helps them have patience and understanding for themselves through time.

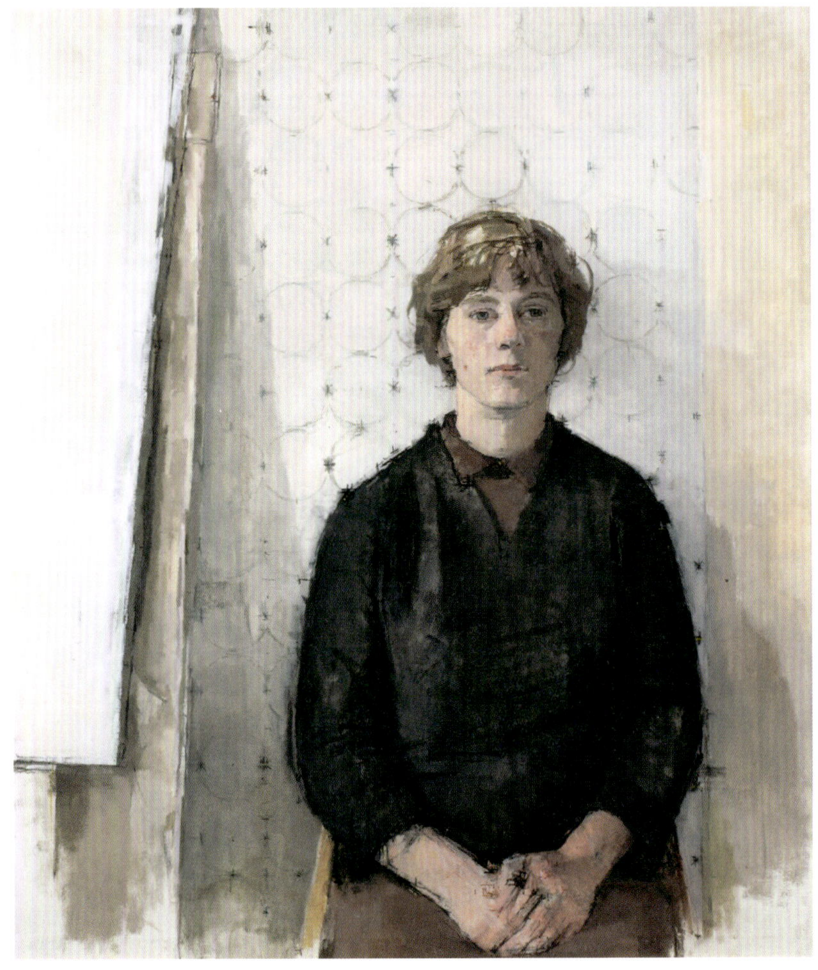

Natalie Dower   1960 · oil on canvas · 122 x 107 cm
Norwich Castle Museum & Art Gallery

LIKENESS

Notes from a lecture at The Slade School of Fine Art, 1967

LECTURES ARE MADE FROM WORDS AND PAINTINGS are not made from words. I have found writing this lecture that the words tend to run away with themselves and generate their own ideas, higher flown ideas than the ones that actually occupy my mind when I am painting.

But now and again I imagine I <u>have</u> found the essence of it all and have hastily searched around for paper to get it down before I forget. Later when I read the essential message the platitude I read is passed belief.

An idea dismissed in a sentence may take a painter a lifetime to explore and the idea may not <u>sound</u> very much.

But at the risk of not making a lecture I have tried to keep the words close to painting.

Painting is about painting and a great deal is inexplicable. I want to talk about what I call 'likeness' painting. What I mean by that may become clear as we go along but even in these pictures of appearance the likeness is only a small part.

At the National Gallery there are very few pictures with this particular likeness. Perhaps only one or two, or some parts of pictures where I can sense the likeness to appearance (where I can believe it <u>looked</u> like that). A visit to the Gallery does not tell me what life looked like for the artists. Most of the pictures are exclusively about art and the outside references seem to me generalisations. Rembrandt and Goya may paint likeness but I think the Rembrandts are about humanity, not about the differences of one person from another. We are not critical, only sympathetic towards all the personalities in the paintings.

Goya's portraits are particular, the people have names and addresses. I look at them with the sort of gossipy curiosity I use watching people come chattering into a lecture hall. The Goyas are <u>transitory</u> likenesses, records of the fleeting appearance, the elusive memory of someone seen once at a party. Nor do I think it is just my imagination that there are so few paintings of likeness (everyday likeness) in the Gallery or out of it. There is plenty to read that cautions the artist against copying appearance.

Baudelaire writing on portraiture in 1846 says there are two ways of understanding portraiture – either as history or as fiction. The first is to set forth the contours and the modelling of the model faithfully, severely and minutely; this does not however exclude idealisation, which, for enlightened naturalists, will consist in choosing the sitters most characteristic attitude – the attitude which best expresses his habits of mind. Further, one must know how to give a <u>reasonable exaggeration to each important detail</u> – to lay stress on everything which is naturally salient, marked and essential and to disregard (or to merge with the whole) everything which is insignificant or which is the effect of some <u>accidental blemish</u>.

So we find that even the history painter is cautioned about painting all that's in front of him. The appearance must first be screened for propriety. The plain look has never been much in demand nor much valued. Nor is it still.

Here is the opinion of the keeper of the National Portrait Gallery, David Piper, writing in an article in the *Sunday Times* supplement: 'A constant preoccupation with portraitists has been the problem of fixing a physical likeness whilst simultaneously lifting the individual out of mere physical likeness into a [nobler] more general sphere, that is in those cases where they ([presumably] the artists) have had the capacity to record more than the mere topography of a likeness.'

The mere topography? Well where are those mere topographies? The plain likeness with no styling?

(Unlike these critics.) So much for art critics. Leonardo says painting is all surface and it is just this likeness of the superficial look that constitutes the magic of representation.

MAGIC

There is magic about capturing a likeness. The fact that you capture a likeness implies that the artist takes something from the sitter.

In rustic countries the country people do not like having their photograph taken. They don't wish to chance giving you their likeness. In case you gain power over them.

Painting somebody does bring about a special relationship between the artist and the model. No one has painted anyone without experiencing the potency in the relationship. The painter seems to gain the ascendency, even though very little may be said. The artist making the likeness does seem <u>to take</u> something.

The Roman poet Lucretius in his book *The Nature of the Universe* writes of the 'skins of appearance'. These he describes as surface films given off in a perpetual stream by the object, sprayed and scattered everywhere. Like the colour from a canopy whose spraying particles [irradiate] the interior. Images flying about everywhere, extremely fine in texture and individually invisible. The painter collects these skins of appearance and exhibits them as his canvas.

As well as the magic of possessing the image of someone there is also magic in the process of <u>making</u> a representation. With nothing more than perhaps a piece of paper and a pencil the artist appears to conjure up a person.

I think some of the pleasure we get is from the effort to make, not the meaning of the strokes. Once we have seen what is being drawn the pleasure is short lived. Instantly one attitude changes from that of being at the mercy of the artist with his mysterious marks that we are at a loss to understand, to being his critic and eager to pronounce whether the drawing is or is not a good likeness. Of course we all believe we know all about a good likeness. And I should think it's true that at sometime in our lives, probably when we were children, we have tried to get a likeness of someone.

Children call all their marks likeness. Hopeless seas of paint or tiny scratches are called things. More or less anything. The names given to these scribbles change but just making a pattern is rare. That single minded concentration is made in the pursuit of the recognisable image. There are ages in the child's life when the artist seems indomitable. But more often he is engaged in a losing race trying to keep pace with the continually increasing demands and his increasing self consciousness.

To some extent you can experience this development painting a portrait. The first simple drawing of the features may seem very like, but introduce some modelling around the cheekbone and so change the style of the description, and suddenly and seemingly inexplicably what was adrift a moment ago is unsatisfactory. In the [new] terms of description the earlier work won't do. This does not mean the subsequent painting is better, the terms are different. The young child's painting may be just as like as the older child's, often more potent because of the directness of the simple style. But the demands of growing up cannot be put off and the child [refuses] and complicates his image by cribbing more complicated schema from his school friends: 'how to do houses, how to do ships'; this is the essential and historical way of learning. And there are recipes in Leonardo's notebooks for how to paint storms. Perhaps a demonstration. And there are pattern books of 'how to do' from Villard de Honnecourt, 1225 [and] to the 'how to do it' series found in every art store.

These flat pattern recipes, that give you a likeness of three dimensions are usually generalisations. You learn to make the dummy and then modify it to suit the occasion. To the child these modifications are made in the light of the constant stream of criticisms pouring in from parents and school and friends. Society conditions you into what's expected and you learn to do what you are expected to do. Child art generally practiced in schools is now an academic art working to certain prescribed rules: sugar paper and self expression.

At home as likely as not you draw your parents. Struggling with the features of their face, anxious that they should concede a likeness. But, in my experience, the drawing is usually not thought to be like, almost certainly you have made the face too old or bad tempered looking. (Who hasn't been told to turn up the corners of the mouth.) Or you may be more helpfully informed that someone has a big chin or wide apart eyes and you then try and incorporate these characteristics in the next attempt.

All artistic judgement given me when I was young was whether a drawing was like or not ('like' being good; 'not like' being bad). As a child I was mystified by these judgements. Not that I questioned them, I tried to get the hang of it all. They came from the grown up world, things had to be learnt all the time, table manners, shutting the door and what constituted a good view.

Sometimes the drawing likeness and the accepted likeness may work the other way around. I had often drawn my face in the glass and I suppose to some extent imagined the drawing's like. But one evening when I was looking at a drawing that had just been done of me I noticed that I had been drawn as someone with a very long face. I remember being a bit put out and only gradually admitting my new likeness. I think I must have <u>almost</u> known that I looked like that, otherwise I would have just rejected the drawing as unlike. But I imagine my discomfort when I saw my likeness must have been nothing compared to the feelings of Charles III when he saw Goya's searing introduction to his face [below].

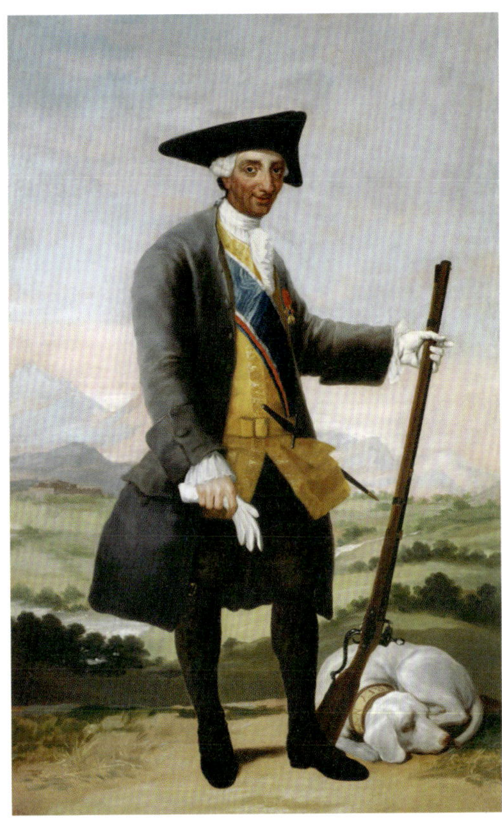

Francisco de Goya
Charles III in Hunting Dress
*c.*1786 · oil on canvas
207 x 106 cm
© Museo Nacional del Prado

EFFORT AND DILIGENCE

You will remember that Baudelaire said of historical as opposed to fictional likeness that the artist must set forth the contours and the modelling of the model faithfully, severely and <u>minutely</u>, so if you could get it all down to the last detail you would have this historical likeness. The fact that it was impossibly difficult and took considerable time only reinforced the idea that that must be the way if only it could be done.

In practice this attitude towards detail was also helped by the inherited tradition of painting. In the fifteenth and sixteenth centuries in Europe the silversmiths, illuminators, gilders and artists were all in the same concern, and the artists practised their skills in a craftsman like way – trying to get in every detail, trying to get it all well finished. Some of [these] efforts to do the imposs-ible (when they did not relapse into decorative detail) produced marvelous and profound statements of what it looked like.

REMAKE

As I see it these painters copying leaf by leaf were remaking the things they painted. There is a way of painting landscapes where first you paint the land then the sky and then put in the tree trunks and branches and hang the leaves [on] the twigs. This seems to me to be painting a description of what you know.

About the structure. <u>The trees stand on the ground in front of the sky</u>. To do this you learn how to make a likeness in paint of the different structures you may require. (People specialise in knowing how to paint houses and boats and flowers ...) and if you wish to make a place for your figures you learn that recipe.

There are five so called [generators] of the three dimensions. Aerial perspective, distribution of light and shade, overlapping of contours, geometrical perspective and interpretation of size. Artists have made up and followed rules dealing with all these phenomena for a very long time. With them they have been able to produce a likeness of three dimensions in their flat canvases. Dürer tells us how to draw Euclid's solids in perspective and Uccello reconstructs the appearance of a Mazzocchio Place. The geometrical base gives a <u>certainty</u> because the theory works, the

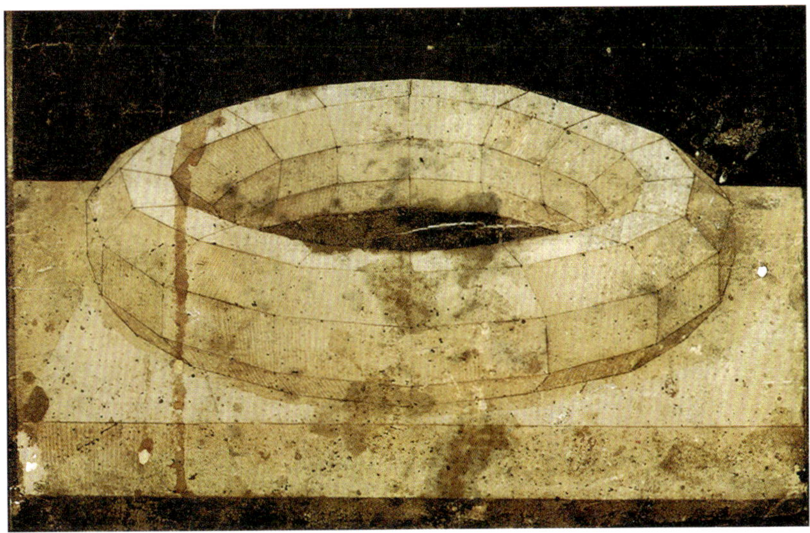

Paolo Uccello · *Perspective Study of Mazzocchio*
*c.*fifteenth century · pen and brown ink and black wash · 16 x 23.3 cm
Louvre Museum, Paris, Departement des Arts Graphiques · photograph in the public domain

result it gives must be how it looks.

Euclid's law on visual rays radiating from the eyes sounded right. So when you draw a chair or stool (there is an early drawing by Uccello of someone sitting on such a stool) and you wanted to give a description of its three dimensions, you made the sides converge towards the eye along the radiating beams of sight.

In this page from a Carolingian manuscript you can see the inverted perspective very carefully calculated to end up at several precise viewpoints. At the bottom left and right. This seemed right, it was a certainty but today it seems an impossible likeness.

ANATOMY

I think the 'how to do it' schema for figures must have made a great advance with the knowledge of anatomy. As an art student I had to study a book called *Anatomy For Artists* produced by University College [London] which makes a particular reference to Michelangelo's anatomical study.

Knowledge of anatomy meant you could remake the likeness

of figures by apparently assembling the physical attributes of humans – you drew the skeleton supported by muscles that levered the limbs into different positions. Like the branches of the tree supporting the foliage so the skeleton supported the flesh which carried the clothes and all the outward appearance.

The general purpose figure was then adapted by what Dürer calls the words of difference. For men this was: thin, fat, soft and hard.

Pictures by Rowlandson and Ardizzone seem to me examples of the generalised drawing of people's bodies modified according to character.

WAXWORKS

These remakes tend to produce theatre type likeness. Character actors in a setting. The pictures were thought of very much as stages with actors. We know that Poussin made little theatres with model figures in which he worked out the arrangements for his picture.

If the model figures get larger they turn into lay figures. The lay figure [flops] around the painting room standing in for the particular people (who may be mythical or too busy to visit the studio).

If you make the lay figures life like you get the figures in Madame Tussauds. As careful collections of the features and dimensions of the face they should be the epitome of likeness. That is the only reason for their existence. With their real life clothes and labelled likeness they persuade us to accept them in their life like terms. But if we jerk away from the calculated display and approach one of them closely then their <u>life</u> likeness disappears. We seem to move nearer a dead thing, a waxy hand looks like a dead man's hand and when we look at the room again we see it full of the dead – stiff in death and rather frightening. Their life likeness now seems death like.

I have looked carefully at one of the faces to test whether looking over the surface of a wax head reminded me of looking across a human face. It does not. I was only reminded of looking at a photograph.

Unlike most sculptured heads they photograph well. I think this is because they have all the accessories, hair for hair, glass for eyes and they are coloured. So the photograph looks like the familiar tonal assembly that nowadays anyway we take for life like.

And they are deceptive. Their smoothness and rounded surface has the same ambiguous quality as illusionist painting.

ILLUSIONIST PAINTING

The illusionist painting sets out to deceive you that it is not a painting. The artist tries to lose the flatness of the board. He tries to prevent the eye from registering the surface. It is not easy to tell where the surface of a very smooth surface lies and the illusionist artist uses smooth flat paint with no brush strokes to catch the eye. In the exhibition at the RA there is a wall hung with illusionist paintings. First year exercise.

The objects are shown clearly illuminated so that they cast strong shadows (that is to say they use the second [generator] of three dimensions). The edges are very sharp. The surfaces of the

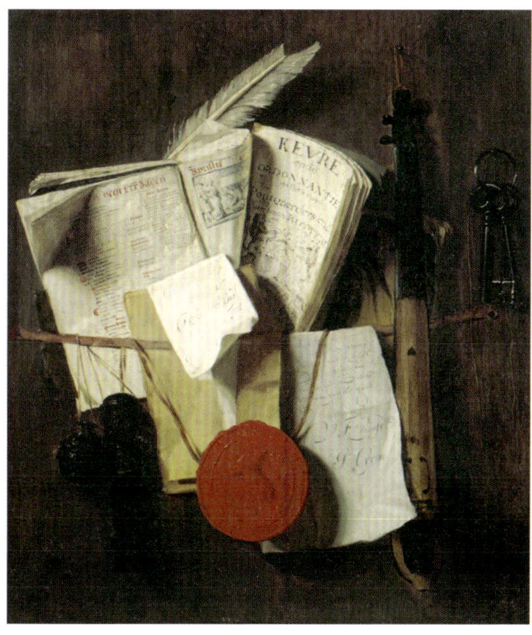

Heyman Dullaert
Still Life
1653–84 · oil on panel
55 x 44.7 cm
© 2019 Kröller-Müller Museum, Otterlo, The Netherlands; photograph Tom Haartsen, Ouderkerk, a/d Amstel

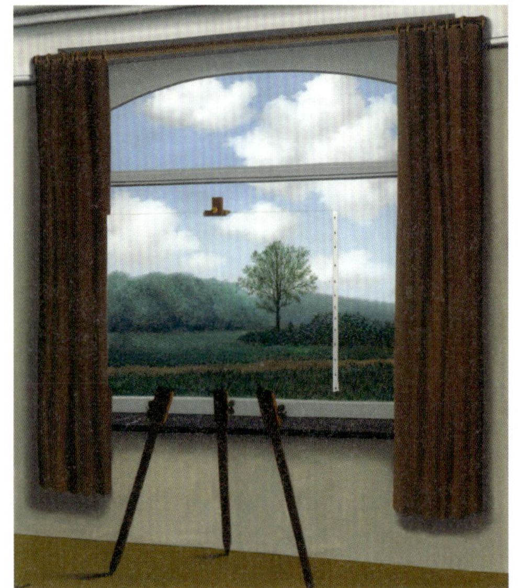

René Magritte
La Condition Humaine

1933 · oil on canvas · 116.2 x 96.5 cm

Collection of National Gallery of Art,
Washington; gift of the Collectors
Committee · © ADAGP, Paris
and DACS, London 2020

objects are often shiny. The progression from light to dark is very carefully controlled: just a small bright highlight within a well lit area, then the side in shadow (the change from light to shadow very carefully blended) and within the shadow a reflected light and then the cast shadow very particularly painted.

If you work hard at the recipe you will get the results.

In illusionist painting we see the likeness of objects but it seems to me a mock likeness, although we may not be able to tell why something seems unreal; to good to be true, the things look like objects nowhere and they exist in a timeless world.

This world of unease was very well suited to the aims of sur-realist painters.

The picture has in itself become a curiosity. A marvel to look at, a demonstration of skill, a trick, a turn or a joke. The likeness carries the joke but it is only a vehicle by which the joke is played.

MATCHING

Instead of conjuring up the likeness you may try to match it. You can do this by placing your board alongside the object or having the object on the board. I believe Picasso had a bird or at least the legs of a bird placed on his board when he was helping his father paint.

In your painting you endeavour to make an exact match of the object (in the same way you might select a tie to match your shirt).

Your painting and the object lie side by side with the surface of the board real to both of them. But another thing that you could do, (imagine for a moment that what you are looking at is the real slice of Mortadella), is to draw a line around it. Then you would have a line that marked out the area the thing occupied, and when the [meat] was removed, you would have at least caught its profile made by the outside limits.

Or you could substitute a piece of glass for the board and place the object underneath the glass and trace the image you saw, or for that matter all the view you saw through the glass like the view seen through a window. For Leonardo this was perspective and Sickert believed this was all there was to drawing from nature.

THE GRID

If instead of glass we put up a grid of wire or strings to look through; and square up the paper in the same units, we can note the latitude and longitude of what we see and put it down in the appropriate lines or squares on one paper. The picture [below] shows Dürer studying a model through a grid.

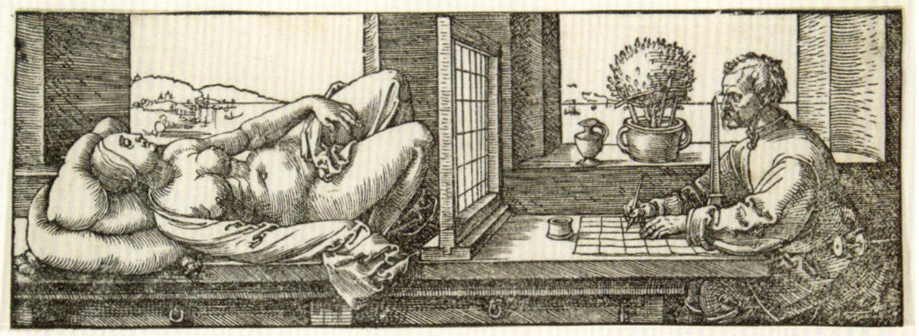

Albrecht Dürer · *Draughtsman Making a Perspective Drawing of a Reclining Woman*
*c.*1600 · woodcut · 7.7 x 21.4 cm
Metropolitan Museum of Art; gift of Henry Walters, 1917 · photograph in the public domain

The view through a grid is special. The mesh running horizontally and vertically has its own beauty and echoes the shape of the page. But it seems to me that the subject is subjugated by this framework. Many artists have used a grid. Surprisingly enough to some people the accredited father of self expression Van Gogh used a grid for a time. There are several references to the grid in Van Gogh's letters, he wrote:

'I have had to pay more for making an instrument for studying proportion and perspective, the description of which is found in a book by Dürer and which the old Dutch masters also used. It makes it possible to compare the proportion of nearby objects with those in a more distant plane in cases where construction according to the ruler of proportion is not possible. And when one tries to do it with the eye alone – unless one is an expert and far advanced – it is always decidedly wrong. I did not succeed in making this instrument at first ...'

And from another letter:

'You must imagine me sitting before my attic window as early as four o'clock in the morning studying with my perspective instrument the meadows and the yard when they are lighting the [fires] to make coffee in the little cottages when the first workman comes [loitering] in.'

Do not underestimate the importance of the idea of a grid or pane of glass on which to record the view. This cut of the cone of vision is represented by the painting on the canvas and is called the picture place. That is the imaginary surface with reference to which the picture takes place, as soon as you consider two positions to appear horizontal to each other it means that you are considering the terms of reference of the picture. For if you move your head in these positions no layers appear to have a horizontal relationship. That eyefull is the limit for those references and it is convenient to think of that area as your canvas or part of your canvas.

The grid gives its truth of likeness. The known verticals and horizontals are represented in the picture by horizontals and verticals. The result is consistent and the pieces fit. But if you try and represent the wide angle of the normal look, you will see the grid itself in perspective. We know that there is only one position:

directly ahead and level with one eye where what is vertical will appear vertical and what is horizontal will appear horizontal. (In the slide you can see this horizontal in the horizon of the sea almost continued in the line of the grid. The stick to which Dürer puts his eye is to ensure that he gets back the same position when the model falls off the table.) On either side and up and down real life parallels will seem to converge. Think of painting the view through a window and the window sill. Looking directly out of the window, the sill appears to curve up on either side. In the likeness made using the grid the sill will be level and things will tend to be made broader the farther they are from the center.

What I find exciting about the idea is that the view comes right back to the person looking at it, like the [slouffed] skins of Lucretius. The appearance of the thing exists all the way from it to you. There is no space, it is packed tight by these [cones] of appearance. Containing the appearance all the way through like sticks of rock with 'Brighton' written wherever you break them.

The view has lost its special everyday look that we necessarily give it to get about among things. Things, and where they are not, are the same. This is important for the artist for that is how they will be on the canvas: marks and areas lying on the same surface.

Paradoxically the effort to hold sight of all the objects all the way back to your eye [enormously] stimulates your appreciation of their real life differences.

THE PHOTOGRAPH

If, instead of catching on our retina these rays of light from the object, we let them pass through a lens or a pinhole onto light sensitive material we have a photograph.

At first the photograph seems like the answer to catching likeness. Impersonally with no particular axe to grind it presents us with the light pattern. Undeniably as it was (at least within limits). The process is quick and the film catches the exact moment it was required to catch. Since photography things have <u>looked</u> different.

We know far more about the appearance that results from movement, appearances hardly guessed at before and that would

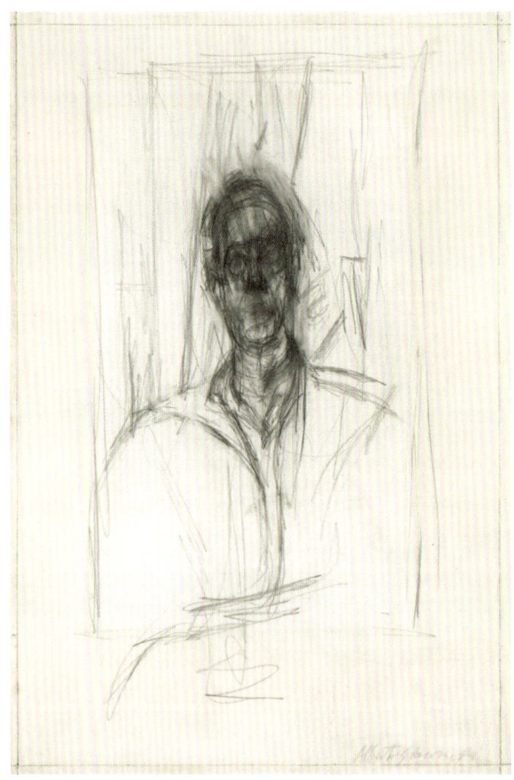

Alberto Giacometti
Portrait of a Man
1948 · pencil on paper
49.5 x 31.6 cm
Museum of Modern Art (MoMA);
gift in memory of Audrey Stern Hess.
Acc. 1364.1974 · © 2020 digital
image, The Museum of Modern
Art, New York/Scala, Florence
© The Estate of Alberto Giacometti
(Fondation Giacometti, Paris and
ADAGP, Paris) · licensed in the UK
by ACS and DACS, London 2020

not have been accepted as like before the camera gave us proof. [Meissonier] is said to have wept when he saw Muybridge's famous pictures of horses in movement.

Now photographic likeness surrounds us everywhere and we accept it as the way the world looks. Rather in the same way that we accept newspaper stories. Only when we have been present at an incident reported by a newspaper do we realise the <u>partialness</u> of the account. And when we see a photograph of a familiar place we may ask ourselves where is it? We can see the features, we can see that must be the opposite hill, and this must be the white house, but why does the foreground slope downhill and why does it all seem so small and far away.

Or have you ever had a photograph taken of the model from where you are sitting? Does the photograph look like what you have been looking at. I find it does not. You can see what the photograph means in its cool and loveless way, rounded and soft at the edges and curiously sentimental.

The photograph is best as a reminder, a snapshot that reminds you of those dreamlike summer holidays on vast expanses of sand or the newspaper photograph of an incident whose dramatic abstraction of a critical second is unique. Like the fatal second for Lorenzo Bandini in his Ferrari [at the Monaco Grand Prix, 1967].

If you move the camera the view changes. Looking through a window with small panes of glass you will see how far they slide over the view if you move your head or jump if you look through one or other eye.

The review reflects <u>your</u> position. Also the things you see are at different distances beyond the glass. If you think of your canvas taking the place of the window then the things will have this spacial relationship with the surface of the canvas. With Giacometti the view takes place behind it. There is a border around the edge which looks where it is [see facing page]. Inside the edge we are taken in until we [come] to rest on the objects.

As we look at the objects in their position we in turn are held by them in our position.

This is not the theatre of *The School of Athens* nor the key hole view of photography. This is single view point painting when the subject is the relationship established by the viewpoint. The likeness is in the looking.

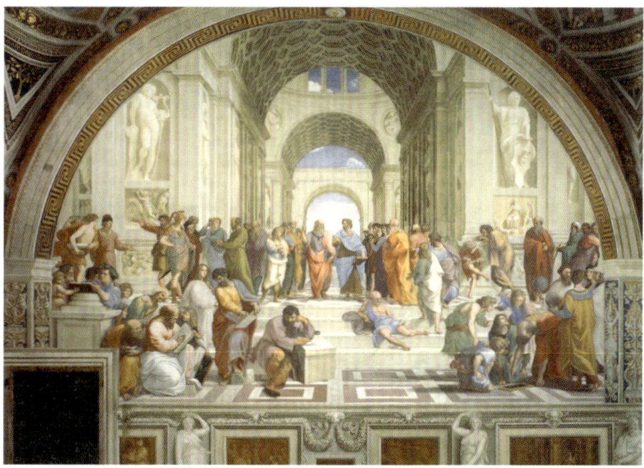

Raphael
*The School
of Athens*
1511 · fresco
500 x 700 cm

collection of Pinacoteca Ambrosina, Vatican Museums; photograph in the public domain

But why this grey world of difficulties? If you want a likeness of the view why not copy what you see in front of you.

Well what is in front of you? Are you quite sure that you can see what's before your eyes. Or perceive it as the psychologists say.

What are you prepared to let yourself see? None of us likes the exceptional. Society is interested in conformity. We are afraid of guessing at what is new and like to cling to what we have already perceived.

According to psychologists we are more likely to see things we can name. If we can't name them then to a certain extent we can't see them.

Try this with colours: you see the patch of sunlit grass and you know it is yellow or yellow green but try to name the colour of the shadow beneath the car. And no name comes up. We don't know what colour we are looking at.

Everywhere we look for meaning. The photograph of a familiar place gave a strangely small hill far away or so it seemed, for we are loathe to accept that distance makes a diminishment of objects.

If you place two candles on a table and one is twice as far away from you as the other then the far candle will appear only half the size of the near one. I always find this passed belief.

Or have you ever been painting a landscape for some time and seen that giant come striding over the fields? Huge, I suppose, because we have overestimated the distance. For the trees to be so big so far away they must be tall trees and the giant surprises us as he quickly crosses the fields we thought so large and walks away among the now stunted trees.

There is a whole range of optical illusions which we fall for each time and even though we are warned we cannot see the falsity.

Artists, I understand, have a lower degree of size constancy than other people. You because of your profession see things differently from other people.

So it is that the farmer sees the landscape differently from the soldier. And the hungry person sees a different view from either the very hungry person (who is apathetic) or the person who is [not] hungry.

And if we are a dog we like to see the doggy things. And our state of _mind_ changes the view. There are levellers and sharpeners and verbalisers and visualisers and some people given to synthetic and others analytic methods of perceiving, and if we are feeling very low and anxious our field of vision contracts.

And there are people worried about their mortgages.

So in a sense no one can see what's before their eyes. But the painter who wishes to find out what is out there has also to describe what he finds. The materials he uses have obvious limitations, the paint is so much duller than light and there are all the practical difficulties: the weather changes, the leaves fall off the trees, hair grows or gets cut, skin gets sunburnt, dresses fall apart. The painter paints trying to catch up on his vision. The vision changes always ahead of him.

The innocent painter imagines he can do anything but leaves off when it leads to the unfamiliar and the bad picture is the one that gives us once again exactly what we had expected.

Michelangelo said that the skill of a great painter is shown in the fear in which he paints a thing and in proportion as he understands it.

The painter sees his subject and wonders what to do and sees his picture and wonders what to do with it, and the state he fears most is to know that something is wrong with the picture but not know what it is. If he knows how the paint marks came to be there then he may know what to do next. Amid the visual confusion he wants answers. But he has to think of the questions to give him the answers. These questions are the artist's procedure.

I would like to discuss the procedure of three artists ...

FRANK AUERBACH

Frank Auerbach says his pictures are not meant to be thick, they come that way. The thick paint results from his procedure.

At each session the picture is painted all over. So that it is always now that is being painted. Now how it looks and now how the picture is to be. (How often have we all felt that we were painting half-heartedly, intimidated by what's on the canvas already.)

Auerbach aims for the accommodating pattern. The concept that will take in everything. If he can find this pattern he may achieve a likeness.

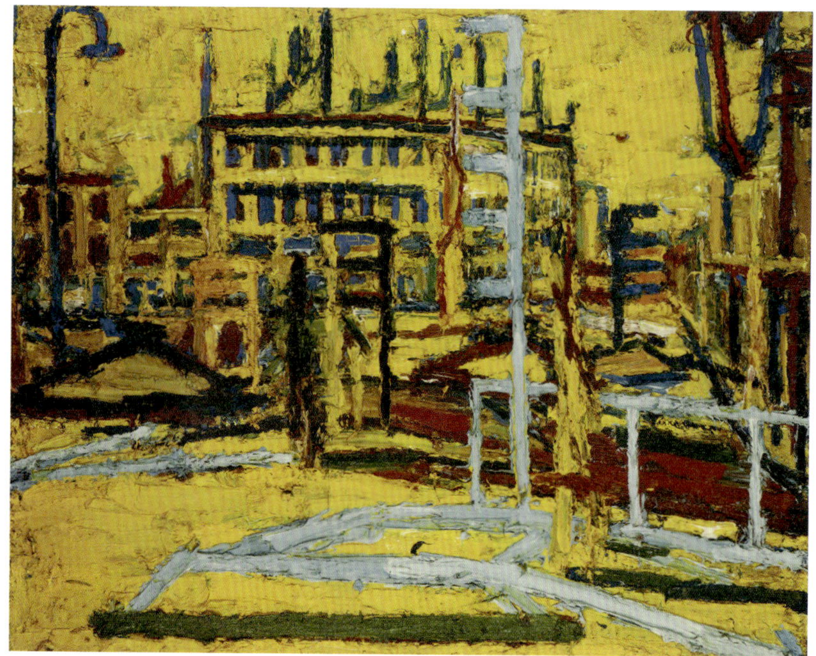

Frank Auerbach
Mornington Crescent with the Statue of Sickert's Father-in-Law III, Summer Morning, 1966
1966 · oil on board · 121.3 x 152.4 cm
courtesy of the artist, and Marlborough, New York and London

Reynolds in his *Discourses* said: 'Nature is multifarious the artist makes a whole of it.' And: 'The great fame of these artists does not proceed from their works being more highly finished than those of other artists or from more minute attention to detail but from that enlarged comprehension which sees the whole object as one, and that energy of art which gives its characteristic effect by adequate expression.'

These pictures by Auerbach seem to me to have a direct relation to Reynolds' ideal of the 'Grand Manner' in painting.

For in these pictures there are no parts, the picture is all of a piece. The image has been painted over and over again, not different pictures one on top of another but each related to what has gone before, and as if of the same family, until the pattern has finally become inevitable, set and finished, is complete in itself like the form of a signature, where the whole shape is recognisable yet the letters obscure.

The all over pattern comes from a visual experience and one visual experience is closely allied to our sense of touch. The child, I understand, first finds out about the nature of his surroundings by testing the relation of the touch of a thing to its look.

These pictures seem to me partly about the way the look can stimulate our physical response, we feel their energy, and partly about the 'all over' going concern of the picture.

As likenesses these pictures are parallel to the thing that is seen – they are analogies. In a sense, Frank Auerbach is a remaker, remaking the physical sensations of the visual image.

The image traced in the glass would be alright if we had square eyes. (Actually that is beside the point) and in fact our retina is concave and even this may be of no account but we do know that one eye is at the apex of the cone of vision.

Large objects near to subtend a large angle. Smaller objects or objects farther away make a smaller angle. We can measure these angles and so form a comparison of their different size – in fact the different sizes and dimensions that the objects appear to be. Obviously to make a comparison of the distances across their cones of sight the measurements must be made at the same distance from the eye. (To a certain extent we can achieve this by holding a paint brush at arms' length and at right angles to one eye.) In this way we can look here and there instead of being bound to the straight [ahead] gaze of the view through the grid. The sum of these measurements will form a roughly concave surface. The disadvantage of a concave surface for the artist is that it cannot be accounted for [on] a flat surface. Think of the various map projections.

WILLIAM COLDSTREAM

[Overleaf] is a portrait of Lord Thomson by Sir William Cold-stream. Coldstream started making maps of people some time ago. His procedure was to gather these proportions of the visual angle. If he could get them he would at least have some answer about the appearance. Answers outside his personal opinions, and in a limited extent, true.

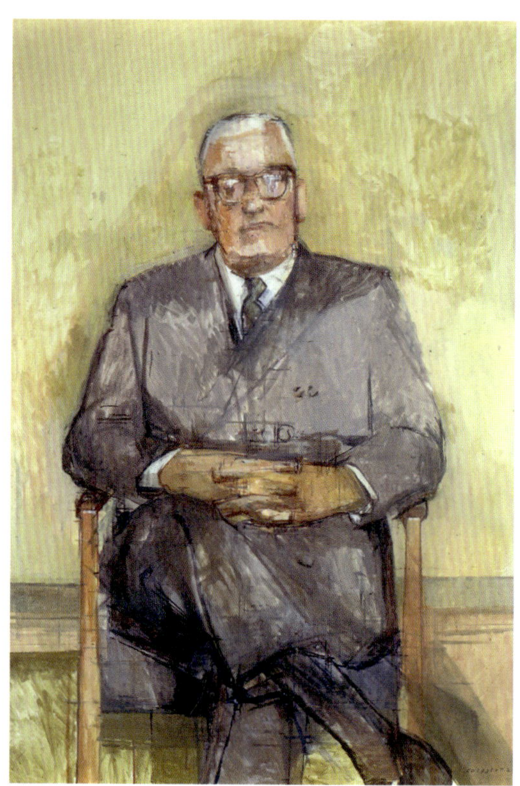

William Coldstream
Lord Thomson of Fleet
1964–6 · oil on canvas · 135.7 x 91.4
International Thomson Organisation

Most painting relies on the artist watching what happens. When something turns up that he recognises and wants, he leaves it. Suppose he is painting an ear, a shape turns up that he recognises as like an ear so he leaves it. But if you are trying to paint what is out there and are suspicious about what you believe you can see and are intent that each mark should present only what you can prove, then, you cannot allow yourself to use the illustration of the thing when it appears on the canvas and in fact, you probably won't recognise the dimensions of the object you are painting when the results of the <u>measurements</u> appear on the canvas.

You may know this passage from the xth book of Plato's *Republic:*

'Does a couch differ from itself according as you view it from the side or the front or in any other way? Or does it differ not at all in fact though it appears different, and so of other things? "That is the way of it" he said: "it appears <u>other</u>, but differs not at all". Consider then this very point. To which is painting directed in every case, to the imitation of reality as it is or of appearance as it appears? Is it an imitation of a [phantasm] or of a truth "Of a phantasm" he said.'

The advantage of seeking the appearance of a phantasm is that you cannot name it 'couch' and do not have perceptions about its appearance.

For the measurements to be compared both the artist and the model have to stay in their respective places exactly. Any movement and a different set of proportions is set up. The model sits motionless, probably after some time uncomfortably, looking unnatural. This is no snapshot, the model looks as if he were sitting to have his portrait painted. He may have to sit in this [hieratic] position for 100 hours or more.

The stillness is not death like because the picture does not pretend to be the glimpse of a moment. The Egyptian Old Kingdom sculptures sit stiffly too. Their life seems compressed by the form that binds them. The figures could never get up, they are not expected to get up, their stillness is the stillness of a gyroscope or an egg.

Why doesn't Coldstream paint on a curved surface? Why does he measure by holding out his arm which [doesn't] pivot at the eye? He told me it was a sport. He was playing a game. On his canvas we could watch the game being played.

These are not scenes from life. They are not illusions. They are accounts. Accounts of a procedure painted on a canvas.

And the likeness is the likeness of the results of an encounter that took place over some time.

EUAN UGLOW

Like Giacometti, Uglow makes the position of the picture plane explicit. With a length of string held at his eye he has arranged it so that the arc the string makes touches the top bar hanging from the ceiling, the nose, breast, stomach and near knee of the model and on the floor at the bottom of the picture a piece of wood.

These points at an equal distance from his eye stand for the uniform surface of the canvas.

This is his premise: this actual surface that he is painting on stands for those equidistant positions out there. Making that assumption the rest follows.

What follows more or less is pear shaped. Uglow likes to be near his model, as near as possible (there is all the difference between seeing the freckles on the skin and seeing the general skin colors from a distance). If you are near and painting all the model you will have to look up at the head and down at the feet and the comparative proportions will be, as I explained with the candles, surprisingly affected by their different distance from the eye and the diminishment this brings about. So you get a pear shape and not a lemon shape partly owing to the distortion caused by the measurements being as the arm sees them pivoted as it is on the shoulder and not centered in the eye. In fact the body does not get smaller.

This effort to catch the phantasm of appearance as viewed by the artist from one position has its own particularities. The picture is of a view and the view depends on the position of the artist and the model. If the model is lying down with her feet towards you then her feet will appear comparatively big. But in fact her feet do not grow larger because she lies down. Uglow to fulfill <u>this</u> condition of likeness changed his procedure for his next painting.

The body was going to be viewed head on. To see each part head on meant that either he or the model would have to move. If the model moved then the background would have to move. So Uglow built a tower and started painting at the feet and moved slowly up the tower shifting his seat seeing by seeing.

<u>I would like to go into his procedure for this picture in some detail to give you an idea of the complexities involved in making, what is called somewhat patronisingly, a life painting.</u>

The unit of proportion in this picture is the length of one of the white tiles seen on the left in the background. The tiles in the picture are painted life size.

Everything else follows, there was no preconception of what was to come. Each rung of the tower represents a different view-

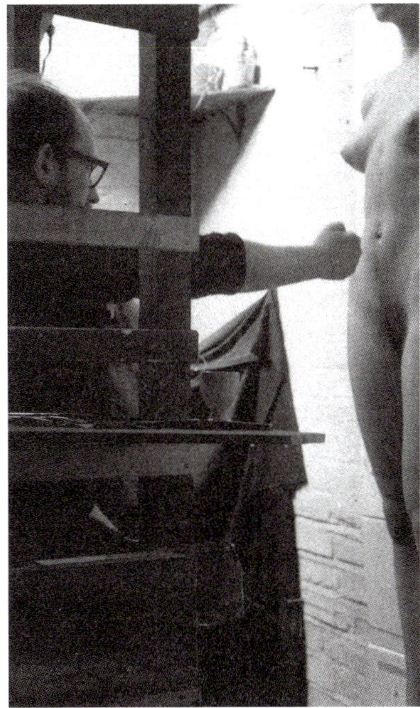

Euan Uglow, *c*.1967

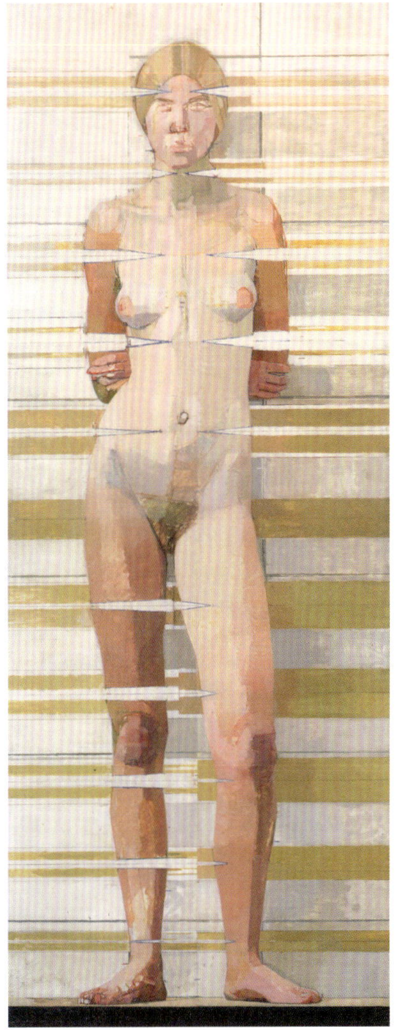

Euan Uglow
Nude, 12 Vertical Positions from the Eye
twentieth century · oil on board · 244 x 91.5 cm
University of Liverpool Art Gallery & Collections, UK/
Bridgeman Images

point. There are 12 viewpoints two to each tile. The picture is
made up of these series of viewpoints one above the other. As
thetiles are life size, and at the edges of each area because she
is nearer, the model will not fit the tile. A position marked on
the model near the edge of one of the fields of view will appear
from the next viewpoint in front of a different tile or a different
position on the same tile.

But the model herself being three-dimensional within her own contours will have some parts nearer than others. Consequently within neighbouring viewpoints an overlap is caused because of the different distances of parts of the limb from the tiles.

Because one leg is nearer than another the overlap of the limb in the background of the farther leg is much smaller than the [rear] leg. (You can see this by comparing the width of the yellow [bands].) The cumulative effect of this diminishment caused by distance would be to make one leg appear actually smaller than the other and the relationship between the two legs would be ridiculous.

To overcome this disproportion the difference is taken between two side by side overlaps and this difference is shown by the gap. This gap (the spear like shapes with [no] paint on) varies in size for the same reasons as the overlap, some of the edges of the limb are nearer the tile than others. The narrower the gap the nearer to the artist, the wider the gap the farther away (see knee in stomach).

Making all these observations the eye has to be kept in exactly the same relationship to the model. The distance from the tiles must be constant and the eye kept exactly in the centre of each field of vision.

Uglow had no idea that anything like this painting would result from the comparatively simple idea that he wanted to paint a model head on and that he would paint the tiles of the background life size. The picture started six feet and has now grown to eight feet tall. He worked out a consistency and let the appearance result from his procedure.

400 years earlier Dürer had speculated over the proportions of the human figure.

The reasons are not the same although the likeness is not superficial. And I do not think it coincidence that although both have studied the appearance of the human figure neither has apparently taken much interest in anatomy.

Dürer says: 'It seems to me impossible for a man to say he can point out the proportions for the human figure: for the lie is in our perception, and darkness about us that even our gropings fail. Howbeit if a man can prove his theory by Geometry and manifest forth its fundamental truth, him must all the world

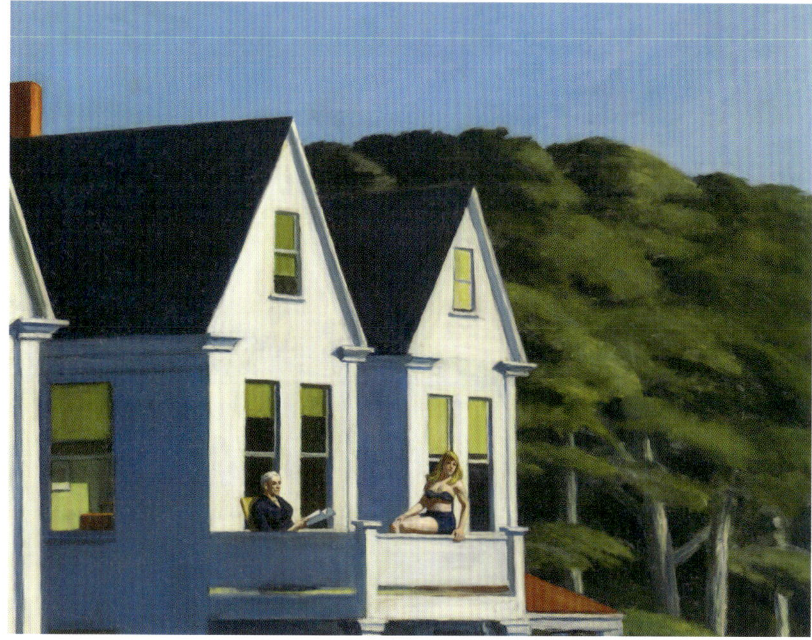

Edward Hopper · *Second Story Sunlight*
1960 · oil on canvas · 102.1 x 127.3 cm

believe, for so one is compelled.'

What counts in all these pictures of procedure is not the intensity of the limitations but the intensity of the artistic process. They are paintings of a process. If you change the procedure you change the subject.

And the belief [rests] with the artist as Wallace Stevens says about poetry: 'The final belief is to believe in a fiction, which you know to be a fiction, there being nothing else. The exquisite truth is to know that it is a fiction and that you believe in it willingly.'

So the artist sets his traps to catch the likeness one way or another – and what he catches surprises him.

This landscape by Dürer still holds this surprise – raw, incomprehensible, unpredictable and authentic. Raw with the edgy green on the foliage, incomprehensible because you cannot make out the physical attributes of the place, unpredictable because you

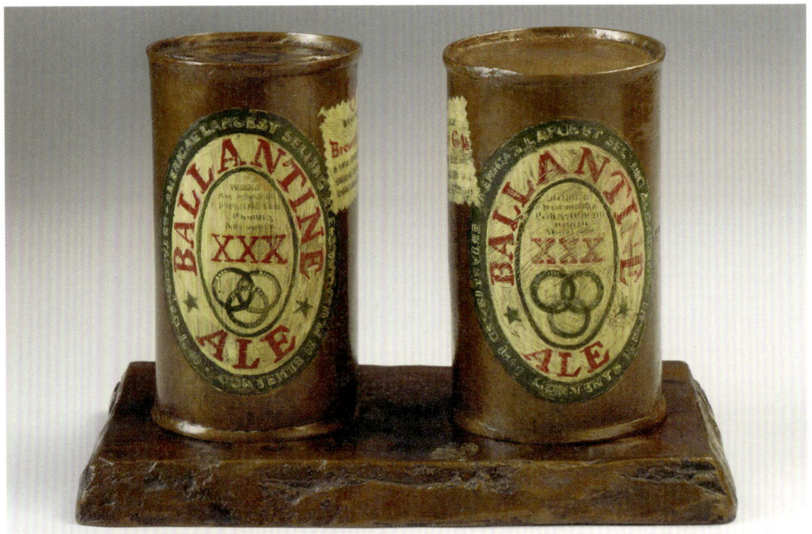

Jasper Johns · *Painted Bronze/Ale Cans*
1960 · oil on bronze
collection of Museum Ludwig, Cologne · photo: © Rheinisches Bildarchiv Köln
© Jasper Johns/VAGA at ARS, NY and DACS, London 2020

just could not foresee that a wall could look like that, and authentic because the message comes through clear and unmistakable and we recognise, without asking why, something we had <u>almost</u> known before.

Equally surprising and equally raw is *Second Story Sunlight* by the American painter Hopper [p. 81], and these beer cans by Jasper Johns [above] are not illusions but monuments. And so is this *Roman Head*. The names of the Roman portrait sculptures are unknown. Makers of likeness have often not been held in much account. For they themselves have struggled with the impossible task of effacing themselves, so that we can see how <u>we</u> look and where we <u>really</u> live.

There is nothing new nor old in making a likeness. We go on keeping our diaries although it has all been done before.

That really is the point.

By cutting notches in a stick or erecting monuments we reassure ourselves we're here.

A likeness helps.

LECTURE NOTES ADDENDUM
Notes believed to have been made in addition to the final lecture

Pictures of reason. Logical painting.

With simple minded determination.

To think clearly and not hide behind the difficulties under a cult of mysticism. If the wall is grey, paint grey whatever *Art International* says. Are going to be logical pictures. Explicable in every case. No question of dullness of [likeness] or expression or [niceness] will come into it. Right answer according to the procedure decided on. And adhered to through ugliness and bad taste.

·

Wallace Stevens: 'What we know fulfils no need at all and what we don't know is exactly what we need.'

·

Goethe: 'The first belief is to believe in a fiction, which you know to be a fiction. There being nothing else. The exquisite truth is to know that it is a fiction and that you believe in it willingly.'

·

Portraits (on Natalie Dower portrait [see p. 56]): The line holding the form – like the string round a bag. Like a lasso – you try and rope it. Catch it. Hold it. The floor. The link between. Primed like a butterfly against the wallpaper. The unit of reality is the O of the wallpaper. Real too is that it has no paint as white is white and equally hopefully the black is black. There is no [contrivance]. The grey [day] normality. The reason for measuring is to find a reason why it is there. The canvas at the back is a canvas.

·

The painting only becomes engaging when the model can keep quite still. Then the measurements may become constant and with their constancy comes belief. The belief that at last some correspondence is growing between the canvas and the model. The canvas at the back is a canvas. Some distance sideways as in depth.

Mr Nicolls commissioned portrait. 40 hours. Not facet cubism. A brasher work. Heather Sutton (portrait). Measuring. Hilary Lane.

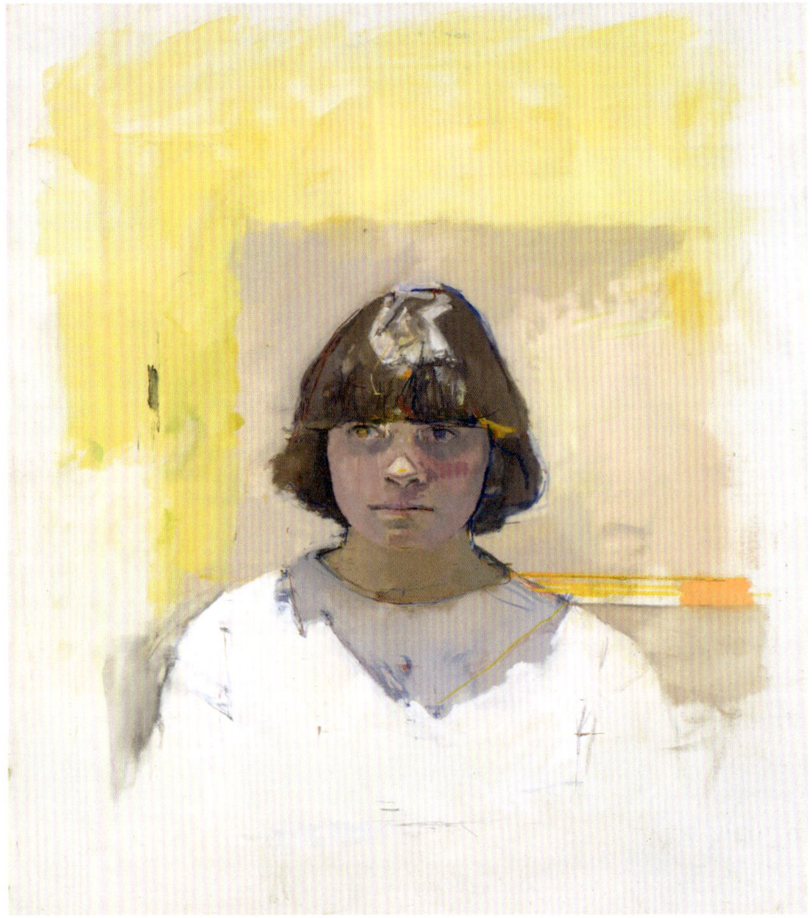

Hilary Lane Night Portarit 1965–6 · oil on canvas · 106 x 91 cm

Night Portrait. Canvas interrupted by the person. Canvas as the field of view. Artificial light, <u>cast shadow</u>. Janice [see p. 18]. The eye. The canvas.

FIRST DRAFT LECTURE NOTES

Including ideas for images not used as part of the lecture

Because the model is three-dimensional some parts are [nearer] than others. Different distances of parts of the body from the background.

·

Consequently within neighbouring viewpoints an [overlap] is caused because of the different distances of parts of the [limb] [from] the background tiles.

·

The point of this lecture is: There are very few likenesses to be seen although everyone has at sometime tried to make one, and it has never been done before.

·

Why my pictures look as they do. And EU's (Euan Uglow's) look as they do.

·

Starting at MF. S [self] and *Les Demoiselles d'Avignon.* The art situation. Picasso, Matisse (Cézanne. And Van Gogh had just been). Learning to like what 'artists' liked. Disliking <u>Cézannesque</u> leads to cubism and style of *Les Demoiselles d'Avignon.* I liked painting what I could see but this was not art.

·

Learnt about <u>Coldstream</u> and watched him painting Auden. / Coldstream sheet. / Matisse was watching. [Peter] [Watson].

·

Almost unknown to us, Balthus was painting his obsessions and his concern with pictures. Balthus friends with <u>Derain</u>, <u>Miro</u> and one of his paintings belonging to Matisse.

·

Working his way amidst the overwhelming stylistic influences coming out of the School of Paris. Making pictures. / Girls and curtain. / Deliberate contrived. / Art Camberwell.

·

Cézanne. Gardener. Does not look the same – [nor] does it seem to lead to. / Picasso Les Demoiselle ... Lost its fear. / Done before S.

Roman Portrait. / Knowledgableness of these artists – art history. A particular stand.

.

Death. Egyptian. Giacometti. / Diary. / Death and the passing moment. /

Awareness – clattering fall of a horse chestnut leaf – never to be stuck back on. /

The sweep of the large second hand on an electric clock. / Who grasps the moment as it flies, he is the proper man.

.

The Flemish paintings sometimes have their own frames. They are small – I take it for convenience for carrying the likeness with you. Real souvenirs. But the frame and the sill hold a different importance for me. Which I shall come to later.

.

Artists have been respected and feared for their abilities to conjure a likeness.

.

The deceptive likeness making has always been part of the art. Perspective: laws to make things seem like life. / The window. With the sill. The marvellous cloth. /

The sill is the front often with lettering which situates the lettering on the surface, some figures lean out. / Rembrandt.

Personal ↓ magic. / Paleolithic cave paintings. / Roman portraits. / Death masks. Wax casts of all ancestors kept as photographs in cupboards are distinct from art. Family portraits. /

Used at the funeral. / 'The Flavian period when [naturalism] in sculpture reached its climax'. / The Antonine artists 160 AD discovered how to reproduce the texture of the skin. / The Roman portrait sculpture only did the head – this was fixed to the bust. / Obsession of likeness [3] Romans. (and death?).

.

From *Autobiography of Vincent Van Gogh.*

Page 63. Concerning the drawing of the figure: '... I have learnt to measure and to observe and to look for great lines. So what seemed to me impossible before is becoming gradually possible now, thank God.'

Page 87: Concerning drawing of landscape in the same manner as the figure: 'I mean especially with a view to the outline, the proportion and the construction; that is
the first thing one has to consider.'

Page 93: 'Bought some beautiful woodcuts from the Graphic.'

Page 113: 'The drawing called Sorrow is in the English style of the Graphic.'

Page 137: 'I have had to pay more for working an instrument for studying proportion and perspective, the description of which is found in a book by Dürer, and which the old Dutch masters also used. It makes it possible to compare the proportion of nearby objects with those as a more distant plane, in cases where construction according to the rules of perspective is not possible. And when one tries to do it with the eye alone – unless one is an expert and very far advanced – it is always decidedly wrong. I did not succeed in making this instrument at first ...'

Page 164: 'You must imagine me sitting before my attic window as early as four o'clock in the morning studying with my perspective instrument the meadows and the yard when they are lighting the fires to make coffee in the little cottages, and when the first workman comes loitering in.'

Page 166: 'First colours. Red, yellow and brown ochre. Cobalt and Prussian blue. Naples yellow, terra sienna, black and white and smaller tubes of carmine sepia, vermilion, ultramarine, gamboge. (This is for watercolour and oil.)'

Page 166: 'Perspective instrument. I have ordered a new and I hope better perspective instrument, that can be fixed on uneven ground in the dunes. I have first come from the blacksmith, who made [it] [on] points to the sticks and iron corners to the frame. The instrument consists of two long poles; the frame is attached to them lengthwise or across with strong wooden pegs. [So] on the shore or in the meadows or in the fields one can look through it as through a window. The vertical lines and the parallel lines of the frame and the diagonal line and the cross, or else the division into squares, are certain to give a few principal points, by the help of which one can make a firm drawing, one which shows the large lines and proportions – at least for those who have some instinct for perspective and some understanding of the reason why, and the manner in which, the perspective gives an apparent change to the direction of the line and change of size to the planes and to the whole mass. Without this, the instrument is of little use and it makes me dizzy to look through it.'

.

Influence of English graphic artists on Van Gogh. Tenniel, Caldicott 70–76, good years. London News. King and [People] 1883. Correspondence with Van Rappard. See *Letters to an Artist*.

Page 262: 'Colour. Looking through the eyelashes. There is something of the mysteriousness one gets by looking at nature through the eyelashes, as outlines are simplified to blots of colour.'

Page 265: Why he is a painter. 'The world concerns me only in so far as I feel a certain debt and duty towards it, because I have walked on that earth for 30 years and out of gratitude want to leave some souvenirs in the shape of drawings or pictures, not to please a certain tendency in art, but to express a sincere human feeling ...'

.

From the *Autobiography of Vincent Van Gogh*. From his letters.

Page 329: First hears about Impressionism 1883 to 1886?

Page 340: Nature seen through a temperament.

Page 341: Colours. And how important it is to know how to use on the palette those colours which have no name, and yet are the real foundation of everything.

Page 400: Colours. Orange, yellow, lemon yellow [chromes], Prussian blue, emerald, crimson lake, malachite green, orange lead, geranium lake ... all the colours the impressionists have brought into fashion are unstable.

Page 421: Without measuring.

Page 429: ... when I come back from the mental labour of balancing the six essential colours.

Page 431: Brings attic for Japanese prints. 100 views of [Fujiyama] Hokusai.

Page 463: Mention of decorative sunflower scheme to Seurat.

Page 536: Copying.

Page 538: Colour. Gauguin and Bernard would say ... They will not ask the correct tone of the mountains, but they will say: By

God, the mountains were blue, were they? Then chuck on some blue and do not tell me that it was a blue rather like this or that, but it was blue, wasn't it? Good – make the mountains blue, and it's enough.

Page XLIII: Enough and more than enough has now been said about painting. It may be suitable to append to these remarks something about the plastic arts. It was through the service of that same earth that modelling portraits from clay was first invented by Butades, a potter of Sicyon, at Corinth. He did this owing to his daughter, who was in love with a young man; and she, when he was going abroad, drew in outline on the wall the shadow of his face thrown by a lamp.

.

Camberwell after the war.

.

The National Gallery pictures were coming back from the mountain tunnels of Wales. We rushed around the continent – learning. / Overflowing with students. Learnt that William Coldstream was teaching there. / One artist who came out of this Camberwell situation was Euan Uglow. Drawing the model – looking at art. Thinking of making pictures.

.

Raphael [?] [Catherine]. / S [Mantigue] steel engravings. Mother of Child. / Rubens Earl of Arundel. / S David. [Bursting] [Sun] and women in the chair. / Elsworth Kelly. Lindner. Giacometti. Balthus. S. / 1) Cubist painting and Ingres.

.

The two standing nudes. 1) S Walking towards. / Likes to be close.

.

The trouble is that things appear smaller farther away. / In fact we know they are the same size. / In this picture each part of the body was to be viewed head on. Uglow moved up the body in 12 stages.

Outline

Alberti. written 1435. Since Painting tries to represent seen things
[let] us observe in what way objects are seen. In the first place when [we]
see an object we say it is a thing which occupies a place.
[the] painter describes this space [we] will call this marking of the edge

The circumstancial changes & difficulties
a landscape outside

Shadows on the canvas

The weather
clouds or no
clouds. Blue
misty or clear
Sunshine or
dark

The sun moving
round during the
day.
The wind blowing the
leaves silver side up
Rain turning the grass
green & the earth dark (insects) getting

the wind blowing the canvas — changing direction
the rain wetting the palette / once bellied
Fog Rain before you begin. It is difficult to see our
cold. Chilly the fingers brain at feet.
Dazzling sunlight on the canvas
The wind ~~blowing~~ the buffeting the measuring arm
eventually impossible to measure. Impossible
a plumb line

& bending the trees into different positions
getting in your clothes or flying round, settling

The farming operations. The fields ripening & then cut —
dunged, harrowed, burnt so the field changes from pa[le]
to dark navy blue. The smoke obscuring the view. The

The outline cuts off one area from another,
The outline usually lies on the ~~body in front~~ edge
the body which is in front.
It is not usually a division but is part of the foremost
body.
The outline falls on the edge or on the last plane se[en]
in perspective.

TEACHING NOTES

A selection of notes prepared for classes
at The Slade School of Fine Art 1956

LESSONS IN DRAWING

The first term. Two mornings a week.

<u>1st lesson</u>: Flat angular paper shapes. Angles on the blackboard. They were to draw them accurately. I had to explain what I meant by <u>accuracy</u>. Unpredictable shapes.

<u>2nd lesson</u>: Paper folded to look like tents. Estimating against ideal vertical and horizontal. Plumb line and ruler. Fallacy of projected image. Leonardo's three columns.

<u>3rd lesson</u>: Lumps of coal. Outline. Measurement. Observed measurement. Similar to circular vision. At least a definite particularity, Dürer. Measurement as beauty in the language of drawing and the other arts.

<u>4th lesson</u>: Lumps of coal and stones. Measurement in the rectangle. Division. Golden section. Placing. Crayons.

<u>5th lesson</u>: Cabbages. Overlapping. Overlapping as an indication of the relationship. To make a space. To place the spectator in this exact position in relation to the scene. Overlapping makes shapes peculiar to painting.

<u>6th lesson</u>: Playing cards. 'Surface is width and length enclosed by lines'. Piero. Lines within the outline to show different surfaces.

<u>7th lesson</u>: Letters and playing cards scattered on table tops. The tendency to rationalise everything we see and the difficulty of objective drawing.

<u>8th lesson</u>: Bricks. Surfaces as planes. By a succession of planes at different angles we get a solid. By drawing the planes edge to edge we get a sense of the solid owing to different perspective of the planes.

<u>9th lesson</u>: Bricks. Matchboxes. Placed in heaps. Seeing the shape rather than arriving at the shape by its boundaries.

<u>10th lesson</u>: Playing cards stuck on lumps of clay. Numerous

planes forming irregular bodies (Masaccio but from nature).

<u>11th lesson</u>: Bottles. The outline and the cross section.

<u>12th lesson</u>: Bottles in groups. The shapes between. Shapes particular to painting. As a help to finding the unprejudiced shape of the objects. Relationship.

<u>13th lesson</u>: 60 odd shapes in clay covered in Plaster of Paris. Shading can show the angle of the surface to the light and there-fore the angle of each surface to the other.

<u>14th lesson</u>: Apples among the shapes. Shading. You are not to draw gloom. As a way of giving more information about what happens within the boundary line.

<u>15th lesson</u>: Plaster casts and a plant covered in white sheets. Loose folds. Explanation of form. Mystery of parcels and what they might contain. Drapery.

<u>16th lesson</u>: Plaster casts wrapped up within the sheets, some sheets wetted so that the sheet followed the surface of the body beneath. Explain the bulk. Make something, somewhere.

<u>17th lesson</u>: Two nude models draped in the same sheets as the plaster casts. On a thing that moves and truthfulness in drawing. The temptation of concocting a plausible image.

<u>18th lesson</u>: Two nude women with the draped sheets pulled tight. The column like person.

<u>19th and 20th lesson</u>: A Banquet. To make the point that life drawing is not regarded as the lessons. Apotheosis of drawing.

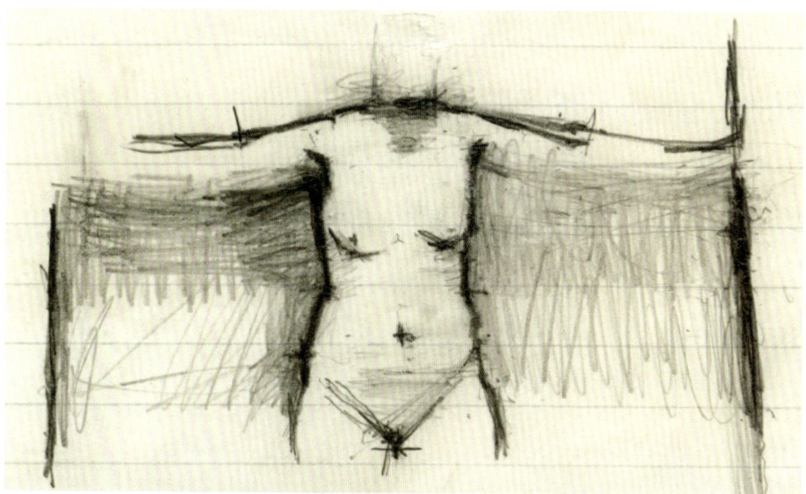

LESSONS IN PAINTING

The second term. One whole day a week.

<u>1st lesson</u>: Materials. Inspection of brushes, palettes, <u>rag</u> etc. That painting is drawing with a brush. Twigs painted in one colour on cartridge paper. The paint stroke not only describing the twig but dividing the page.

<u>2nd lesson</u>: Tone. Bright coloured paper of various shapes stuck all round the room in a frieze. Asked to paint the shapes in their relative tones using only a dark pigment and white.

<u>3rd lesson</u>: Red, yellow, blue. Called primary coloured pigments. That colour can be seen as a deviation from grey. Grey comparatively true in same way as lines are comparatively true.

<u>4th lesson</u>: White Bricks. Warm lights, cool shadows. Influence of light on colour.

<u>5th lesson</u>: Heads in planes. That a round form like a head can be explained on canvas on the flat by a series of flat planes.

<u>6th lesson</u>: Pipes of all sizes from drain pipes to one eight feet long. The difference between the flat canvas and a cylinder.

<u>7th lesson</u>: Light globes. Billiard balls, ping pong balls. All white. The difficulty. Painting a record of statement by the artist.

<u>8th lesson</u>: Flowers. Colours as colours in their own right. Red is red, etc.

<u>9th lesson</u>: Two nudes. To establish some sort of connexion between these classes and what is done in the rest of the school.

COPYING

Two whole days a week in either the Tate or National Gallery. The students have been asked to study the pictures not as painting a picture of a picture but to paint from the picture in the same way as they would paint from an apple.

SHAPES

Lines containing a shape. The bounding lines cut off the enclosed area from the rest. So the lines not only have their identity – one line to its neighbour – longer or shorter and at various angles but linked together [contour] something quite apart from themselves, a shape. Usually before you identify the lines you recognise the shape – the lines are auxiliaries – <u>they</u> are a sign. The shape exists, <u>the line does not</u>. It marks the boundary.

Because you see and recognise the shape. You are reminded of a square or diamond or pentagon – there is a tendency to draw just that without attending to the particular characteristics that the lines describe.

The difficulty about finding out what a shape looks like is that one is so sure that one sees <u>a shape</u>, that one is determined to make the lines link up in a plausible way.

You have to try and find out what things look like – you have to try and see beyond <u>your preconceived</u> views.

.

Shapes and the fact that divisions make shapes on either side. A line divides and on either side there is a difference. In real life there are objects surrounded by air and although we cannot usually see the air, except for fogs or the atmospheric mist seen between us and at distant objects, our experience makes us realise that it is there.

.

When we draw an object on a page the world is reduced to two dimensions so that the object and the space are described in a similar way. The line shows the boundary between the object and whatever is behind the object. The object and its measurngs have been reduced to two defined areas adjoining each other. At the same moment and with the same line we have described the object and what is behind the object. Usually this line is the boundary between two shapes although you can imagine that in a drawing of a chair placed before a large bare wall the shape of the wall surrounding the chair will be difficult to appreciate as a shape and in fact its shape will be an entirely artificial one made by the limits of the canvas.

The lines in this case will seem to rest in the limits of the chair although of course they will also describe where the wall is interrupted by the chair. More often the line will divide two shapes which although very different in real life – that one corresponds to the limit of an object and the other appears to be a quick arbitrary cut of something by chance behind the object, when reduced to the terms of drawing become shapes with very similar characteristics.

·

Leonardo: 'The boundaries of the bodies are the least of all things. The proportion is proved to be true because the boundary of a thing is a surface, which is not part of the body contained within that surface; nor is it part of the air surrounding that body, but is the medium interposed between the air and that body.'

·

Piero: 'Within the convention of drawing, without the lines the shape could not exist on your page.'

·

The difficulties of seeing clearly – the dodges, lines running through identified a conventional shape, that is to say a shape that fits in with your vocabulary of familiar shapes … is a square, a diamond.

Yet we are not interested in what we know, only in what we do not know. We must face these objects and try to forget all we know about them and about the things they remind us of.

·

Drive the lines as I have asked you. Train your pencils like Ruskin's well trained horse. Start with a length and to that add another length. Keep your mind on the shape but your eye on the line. Try to be so naive in your drawing that you risk not joining up at all. When you go back to your first length draw slowly and deliberately. Make clear that a line is the demonstration of a decision. A clear mark of a certain direction and length. Obvious progression shows the effect of distance on size and the effect of angle on shape.

Interesting to notice how the squares get so much smaller further away. That is why they are squares. And how it is very hard to believe some of the thin shapes facing you are in fact squares.

Consider a piece facing you as parallel to the surface of your page. Then the other pieces are parallel or inclined. You can easily recognise their inclination by their brilliance. The brightest being that directly facing the light.

Start again at the front of the page with the point [and] side of the object nearest to you.

SHAPES NEXT TO SHAPES

Shapes peculiar to your position. The shapes made on the page describing the object will often be very unexpected owing to perspective. There is another shape particular to drawing. The shapes made by the edges and corners of the page are the lines. The lines will describe the limits of two shapes lying on either side, divide the page or perhaps make a division of the page from edge to edge. How the artist manages this will help or hinder the explanation of the scene.

.

Shapes come next to shapes and make a collection of notes each relying on the other, these by their density make a corporate body. To draw the body. These shapes are further distorted from their intrinsic shape by overlapping.

Yesterday there were shapes and a surrounding area. In fact this is rarely the case.

Shapes lie against shapes. The line is the common boundary. In one stick we define two sides.

.

A conscious appraisal of what we usually do without analysing all actions. Flat shapes. Seen as area – drawn as area – lines used to describe the area but not considered as flat shapes. The phenomenon of lines joining to cut off a piece of paper from the rest. A shape. Something apart from the lines but made by the lines. The shape is real, the lines are a sign. Boundaries.

It is very difficult to see their shapes because you know what to expect and we always tend to rationalise what we see. Because you know there are squares you will tend to draw squares.

.

Seeing shapes as shapes rather than linear boundaries.

The shape is real, the lines are a sign. The marks of drawing, the description. Going back to the first shape in the same way as you went back to the first line. Arriving at the shape. Boundary line common to both. Like a party wall.

(Black paper folded and taped to the walls some white paper pinned to grey screens.)

The shape is more than the sum of the boundaries. Think from the middle.

Consider correspondences of side contains surfaces and [leave] shape recognition with [line].

.

Lines ... decide on the shape. Make a similar shape on the page – compare the two and alter the shape you have drawn until it resembles as close as you can the shape you see. Draw the next shape. It will condition the first shape, especially their common boundary. See that together they form a third shape that encloses them both. Draw this shape – it will condition both the smaller shapes – go on expanding. Flat shapes in a mosaic. Shape beside shape, field next to field. Making a surface.

Go back to the first shape again and again. Show the progression from position to line to sequence of directions and space between to contained space between.

The page as space. So if you leave a great deal of white paper it stands for a certain volume with nothing in it. Size standing for distance, near things big.

ACCURACY

Today I wish to make clear what I mean by <u>accuracy</u>. It is important whether you are drawing from an idea or an object to state exactly what you mean. You know how difficult it is to draw a face that looks like. Any small deviation in the balance of the features and it looks like someone else or nobody at all. Points which explain positions. Lines, a series of points that have a certain length and direction.

FALLACY OF THE PROJECTED IMAGE

The picture plane is an imaginary barrier crossing the line of sight between you and the object. The image of the object is projected on the picture plane. The picture plane represents your piece of paper and like your sheet of paper is flat. Your drawing represents the image cast on the picture plane.

The painters of the Renaissance believed that by having something transparent between yourself and the object and tracing the image, they were imitating the nature of appearances. To a great extent they were right. Northern artists followed their examples, Dürer with his grid [and other measuring instruments] – [Holbein], [Sickert].

The grid before the object and similar squares of the page.

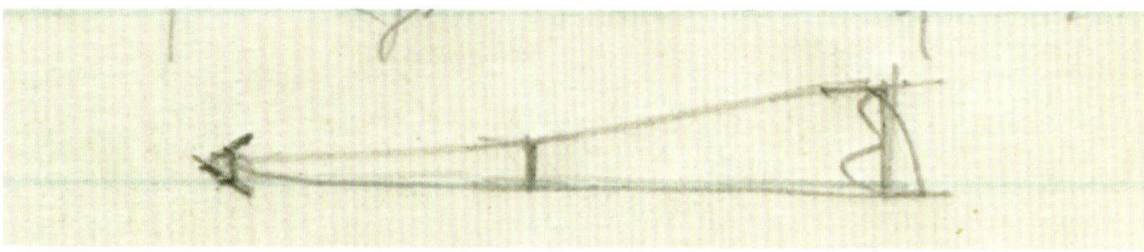

But Leonardo realised the fallacy of this. The plumb line is one vertical from a grid and can be proved to have its limitations. Nevertheless, unless you are willing to admit that there are [no] straight lines it has some value in correcting the errors of your eye.

DOWELS

Arranged on the brown paper are pieces of wood called dowels. They are of various lengths. You will find out by looking at them the different lengths and how they are related. None touches the other. The gaps between are as important as the lengths of wood – like the silence between the notes of music.

I want you to concentrate on drawing the length in their right proportions – in proportion to the other pieces of wood and in proportion to the space between. Perhaps it would be best to draw the pieces of wood as lines, just select a piece of convenient length – then compare <u>the neighbouring piece</u>. <u>It will be either longer or shorter or the same</u> and its distance away will be judged by the length of the first piece. You must get it exactly right. Exactly. Or like a bad fiddler you will be out of time.

You will also have to compare the angle the pieces have to each other, and you must ask yourself, is this piece tilted more to the left or the right than its neighbour or are they parallel? I really do want you to ask yourself these questions and for the drawing to do the answers. Keep going back to the start and progressing again and again until you have the lengths and dispositions just right.

These objects look very simple but remember that Michelangelo said: '... and the skill of a great painter is shown in the fear in which he paints a thing in proportion as he understands it.' Be fearful.

DOWELLING [HUNG] UP ON [COTTON]

Here are the same pieces of wood. Suspended away from the wall. The angles they make to your eye are those both of their own in relation to gravity and each other, and they are caused by the relationship between them and your eye.

It is for the first time very important where you are. If you move the pattern changes. Your drawing is describing where you are.

The actual measurement of the pieces of wood is of little help to the drawing. Their apparent size is determined by the angle they lie at to your eye. From elevation to end on. The smaller the pieces appear in relation to their actual length, the more they must be turned away or towards you.

The page is flat, you have to see the lengths of wood suspended in space as flat images before you can translate them into the terms of your page. If you do this successfully then the pieces of wood will appear to have a three-dimensional relationship with each other and the page will give the illusion of being a three-dimensional space.

Some of the bits are nearer than others. So their apparent size not only determines their angle to your eye but may also show their distance from you. If you move your head, the dowls alter position. Sideways or up and down. So you not only describe the position of the piece of wood in space, but also your own position which the dowels reflect.

The paper is no longer the same. Its surface is dissolved it is an infinite cavity into which you put things and there things describe its extent.

Imagine the nearest piece of wood to be lying on the surface of your page. Relate the other pieces to it going back [in] the appropriate intervals. Angle and size of the pieces of wood hung up so their distance from you and their angle to your eye will alter their familiar shapes. They are equilateral triangles and squares with a few exceptions.

.

The actual size of the drawn object to the
size of the sheet of paper.
1. The things. Lengths. Length determined
   not only by themselves but position.
2. Yourself. Move head. Precisely describing
   your position.
3. The page.

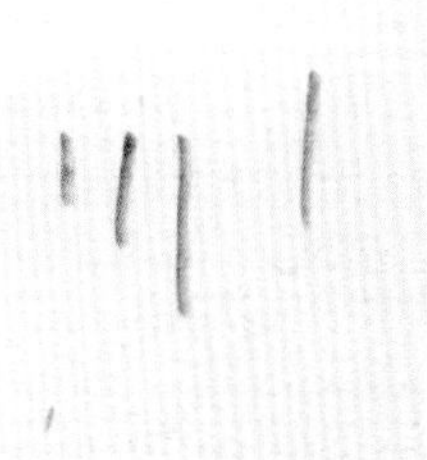

.

The influence of distance in length Lengths appear smaller further away. Size of the pieces determined by their actual size and their distance from your eye.

Or because large things appear nearer and smaller things farther off. The smaller you make a thing, the greater the distance you will have described between your eye and the thing.

PLANES
Piero said: 'Surface I say, is width and length enclosed by line.'

Oxford Dictionary says a plane is: 'Surface such that the straight lines joining any two parts in it lies wholly in it. <u>Lines within an outline usually show a change of plane</u>.'

These are the shapes of the last lesson, two-dimensional stuck to the wall. You were showing how lines linked together formed a shape – they isolated an area from their surroundings. But the lines often imply not merely an isolation but a description of the type of shape they contain. Last week you drew outlines and inferred what lay within. Today the outlines will describe the surface of the thing they contain.

In the same way that the angle to your eye and the distance from you modified the apparent angle and size of the pieces of wood hung up, so their distance from you and their angle to your eye will alter their familiar shapes. They are equilateral triangles and squares with a few exceptions. It is very difficult to appreciate that squares can appear long and thin – in some cases as thin as a piece of string.

Nor only in fact, through the language of lines joining each other and various angles and with various proportions with all the energy they seem to display, you must show the relationship of angle, of tilt of one plane to another – of one to its neighbour – each complimentary to the other and together forming your opinion of the next, until you have a collection of planes on your page, each aware of its position and inclination compared to all the others. Consider your page – remember on your page you can have nothing, but an assembly of lines.

·

A plane is a shape but more particular.

The apparent size of an object depends on how much of your field of vision it occupies and proportionately to other objects. Remember the enlarging pattern.

1 defines 2. 2 is 2 because 1 is 1. Together they make 3. Recognise 3.

Drawing is not that 1 defines 2 and 2 defines 3 and 3 defines 4 or even that 1 and 2 define 3 or 1 and 2 and 3 define 4.

The importance is to see the cumulative shape. Neither is drawing starting by guessing the total and dividing down its units.

·

<u>Planes. Tilted yet another way</u>. Black squares. Postcards. Seeing it flat. Look at your sheet of paper and mentally move your hand across it. Your lines not only isolate the shape from the surrounding space but describe the type of shape they contain.

A line suggests the area it bounds. Lies in the same plane as the line itself. Make planes at all costs. Make shapes similar to the shapes you can see considering the likeness of area rather than an enclosure of lines.

If an occasional line be out of tune you will also have to compare the angle the pieces have to each other and you must ask yourself the question; is this piece tilted more to the left or the right than its neighbour or are they parallel.

I really do want you to ask yourself these questions and for the drawing to be the answers. Keep going back to the start and progressing again and again until you have the lengths and dispositions just right.

THE PICTURE PLANE

Now hanging in space they are shapes still but with the particularity of planes. Planes have some relation with the flat shapes you were drawing earlier on.

Drawing the space. Front to back of the page. On a page big things look near.

One way of correcting the errors of your eye is by comparative measurement.

Drawing is the putting it somewhere and getting it right, in this case right to how it looks. The predetermined drawing. Right to show how a drawing looks. How can you get out of this repetitive situation. Overlapping. In between shapes particular to painting and drawing. These shapes have three-dimensional boundaries and are the connection between one object and another. It is possible to draw the objects by drawing the space they leave. This is perhaps a negative approach but one is less prejudiced about shapes than about objects and description of the shape between is of use in finding out what the object looks like.

.

Apply a principle. The unrecognisable marks. Corbusier: 'The establishment of a standard is developed by organising rational elements, following a line of direction equally rational. The form and appearance are in no way preconceived, they are a result; they may have a strange look at first sight. [Ader] made a 'Bat', but it did not fly; Wright and Farman set themselves the problem of sustaining solid bodies in air, the result was jarring and disconcerting, but it flew. The standard had been fixed. Practical results followed.

.

Remembering the enlarging pattern:

1 defines 2. 2 is 2 because 1 is 1. Together they make 3. Recognise 3. Drawing is not that 1 defines 2 and 2 defines 3 and 3 defines 4 or even that 1 and 2 define 3. Or 1 and 2 and 3 define 4. The importance is to see the cumulative shape. Neither is drawing starting by guessing the total and dividing down into units.

It is unlikely that the piece nearest you is lying parallel to you. So only one end will lie on the surface of your page You will drive your pencil back along the pieces probing the blankness of your page and transforming it into space.

.

The [mental] effort to bring compatibility to the side of the table leg seen against the line and the edge of the line running away from the eye seen as a diagonal.

Or it is seeing the end of a box as a diamond. There is no doubt one is usually very surprised to find how a picture turns out. For the very reason that one had no idea what the subject looked like flat.

.

An imagined screen between you and the object. Represented by the surface of the page.

Imagination. / Ruskin. / Progression. / Proportion. Unit of measure. / Direction. / Angle. Unit of angle. / The module.

Drawing as a logical succession. You not only describe the thing but its positions in space. / Seeing them flat. Translation into the two-dimensional term of the paper.

SEQUENCE OF PLANES

Loss of the emphasis on outline. The planes are outlined but since you will select which planes you draw it is possible that the objects will not be outlined.

The outline has no more significance than that they are the line defining the limits of the last visible plane in the object.

Drawing the planes including the surface of the table. / Measuring using arm and pencil.

TWIGS

Shapes. Twigs interlaced. Taped back. Branches mostly in two dimensions taped to the walls. The phenomena of the lines meeting and so cutting off an area, a shape.

To make the drawing travel from a point, the point of departure is a direction to change. Direction and travel for as far farther or for a shorter distance to change direction and to travel again a relative distance until the line may meet the point of departure and so isolate an area, a shape.

The twigs are more complicated but I wish you to translate them into the same sort of terms. Here it is more complicated to translate them into the same terms as you used when you drew the pieces of wood. The twigs are meant to be just in two dimensions. Also get the beauty of the twigs. Make the drawing grow like a twig, the same jerky deliberate movement. This growth with strength.

You must be very careful to insist on the same sort of accuracy. Even though this means drawing very slowly indeed. Start with a convenient length and progress. Ask yourself where shall you make the pencil travel and give yourself simple but clear directions. Somehow or other you must extract the <u>beauty</u> of the twigs. Their particular beauty is a matter of extreme precision.

.

How length is determined by distance, by angle, by cut.

Three-dimensional space.

Some of the bits are nearer than others, so their apparent size not only determines their angle to your eye but may also show their distances from you. It will now be more difficult to see how these things look because we tend to rationalise them into their known qualities. We attempt to pull them from their unusual angles to an elevation which is their most characteristic. So that the long pieces of wood we know to be longer look longer than the short pieces. The apparent lengths of the wood are no longer absolutely determinable.

You will have to watch the relationship of the angles. You will watch the angle that you imagine these things make to each other in real life and translate that into the flat angles that the lines will make on your page. It is the seeing what they look like flat that is difficult. If you can do that, you can make the things stick out just as they appear to do – or nearly. Description. Exactness. How to hold the pencil. As a development of the way you have been seeing.

MEASURING

Piero said painting consists of three principal parts which we name drawing, measurement and colouring.

Observed measurement. / Comparison of one size to another.

·

You will hear people asking how to make a thing stick out. It is a matter of proportion as the Renaissance discussed and as the Northern artists Rembrandt and Dürer found out from Italian painting.

·

How to hold the pencil. The awareness of the picture plane. Measuring as a way of reinforcing picture plane.

A system of comparisons. / Use no rubbers. Draw lightly at first. But clearly a plain line. / Choose a convenient length. Neither the longest or shortest. Choose one eye. / Write this on the sheet. / Guess first, measure afterwards. / Sharp pencil. / Measuring – reminder of the picture plane. / Lying the pencil along an angle.

·

Length is affected by the angle the object [subtends] to the eye. Foreshortening.

Size of the object is more determined by its actual size, distance away. Sight size is the size of your drawing when the drawing hand is in the usual position it is apparently the same size as the appearance of the object. It depends entirely on how far your drawing is from your eye.

OUTLINE

Projected image. For account of the outline. Picture plane, imaginary horizontals and verticals. / Plumb lines and horizontals.

Meeting place of space and the object. The line cuts out the body from the space.

·

The simplest way of illustrating something is by drawing an outline profile. Primitive drawings – cave drawings of animals.

The outline usually lies on the edge of the body which is in front of another. It is not usually a division but is part of the outline falling on the last plane seen in perspective. In itself it is three-dimensional like a succession of the pieces of wood you drew last time. It will come nearer or go back.

The outline cuts off one area from another.

You can imagine the same succession of proportions around the edge. You will start with how you can check the errors of your eye. Verticals and horizontals. You can compare the points to something they have in common – gravity. Compatibility of verticals and horizontals with the rectangle. Important to realise the difference of real objects.

.

Alberti: 'Outline will be that which describes the going around of the edge in painting... I shall wish that nothing be attended to in circumscribing [but] the going along of the edge. I assure you that in this great care [must] be exercised. No composition no illumination describes [praise] unless there is good circumscription in addition. And good drawing, that is good circumscription, is often pleasing on its own account.

.

Since painting tries to represent seen things, let us observe in what way objects are seen. In the first place when we see an object we say it is a thing which occupies a place. The painter describing this space will call this marking of the edge with a line circumscription or outline. Then looking it over, we observe that many surfaces in the seen object connect, and here the artist, setting them down in their proper places, will say that he is making the composition.

.

The question as to the origin of the art of painting is uncertain. The Egyptians declare that it was invented among themselves six thousand years ago before it passed over into Greece – which is clearly an idle assertion. As to the Greeks, some of them say it was discovered at Sicyon, others in Corinth, but all agree that it began with tracing an outline round a man's shadow and consequently that pictures were originally done in this way, but the second stage when a more elaborate method had been invented was done in a single colour and called monochrome, a method still in use at the present day. (Line-drawing was invented by the Egyptian Philocles or by the Corinthian Aridices and the Sicyonian Telephanes.) These were at this stage not using any colour, yet already adding lines here and there to the interior of the outlines;

hence it became their custom to write on the pictures the names of the persons represented.

·

1) Circumscription. 2) Composition. 3) The reception of light.

Outline will be that which describes the going around of the edge in painting ... I should wish that nothing be attended to in circumscribing but the going along of the edge. I assure you that in this great care must be exercised. No composition, no illumination, deserves praise unless there is good circumscription which is often pleasing on its own accord ...

·

Piero della Francesca: 'Painting consists of three principal parts, which we name drawing, measurement and colouring. By drawing we mean profiles and outlines which contain the objects. By measurement we mean the profiles and outlines placed proportionally in their places.'

·

Drawings being pictures. No such thing as studies. That the drawings should be descriptions of the situation before you. The horizontals found by a spirit level can be found to be arcs moving upwards.

LETTERS

A diversion from the white shapes.

The further the angle of the thing we see differs from our imagined picture plane, the more difficult it is to make the translation from the object to the page.

·

You are faced with a table full of letters. Nothing you see is parallel to your picture plane. The plane of the table is running away from you like a landscape seen from a hill.

I have scattered letters on the table because letters are some of the shapes you are most familiar with. Usually you look at them only to find out their literary meaning. But in almost the same way you look at everything. Like an illustrator, someone who draws, and to make his meaning clear he usually draws things by their well known symbols. I want you to try and find out how the letters actually look to you. You will try to make an A look like an A, but perhaps before you will be able to see it, and so to draw it lying on the table you will have to forget that it is an A.

LETTERS AND BRICKS ON A BLACKBOARD

By small shapes explaining the layer. The letters playing cards and bricks, all very familiar objects. Lying on a horizontal plane (at the greatest angle to the picture plane) they are most difficult to see.

The bricks have planes contained within their contour. Explain the surface of the board using the letters and bricks: draw the objects which by their common denominator will draw the blackboard. Let the sum of the objects explain the surface. The objects as numbers. Keep an eye on proportions.

CUBES AMID LANDSCAPES

Planes joined up to form a solid. / The same white planes that you have seen before, but be aware they now join to form a familiar object and it is only too easy to disregard their appearances and draw a brick.

You knew about letters and found how tricky they were to draw – now be on your guard when you look at these familiar bricks. / There are the first objects you have drawn that have planes at different angles within their contours.

The lines inside the outline show where the planes change their angle.

.

Selection.

In drawing a plane inclined towards you – you have to pull the far boundaries forward and push the protruding edges back so that all things meet on the plane of the drawing.

It is the incompatibility of receding planes and the plan to be made of them on the page that prove the crux of drawing. To be able to translate the visible world into a plan or map is to be able to draw. You have to pull the far boundaries forward and push the protruding edges back so that they meet on a common plane, an imagined plane of the picture. And putting it right. In this case right to how it looks.

The farther the surface to be drawn is inclined from the eye, the more difficult it is to translate what is [seen] into the terms of the paper.

You have to translate this scene into a map. I have often spoken about lines being marks on the paper and that you should be aware of the lines and marks and of their relationship to the side, top and bottom of the page. So the question is bound to arise, is some place better than another on the page?

.

Oscar Kokoschka, School of Vision [Salykug], 1954: 'Vision, and the ability to give it form comes naturally to the child. But this faculty withers as we grow up ... It is, therefore, not a question of learning technical skill or photographic reproduction in my school ... I want to teach my pupils the art of seeing, which has been forgotten today.'

THE GOLDEN MEAN

You can divide your page and the division can have some re-lationship to one of the sides. You can divide it half way and a quarter so that the length is the length of the hypotaneuse of a right angle [in] the division is [as] one of the sides or in the Golden Mean, which is an off centre division where the smaller unit is to the larger as the larger is to the whole.

These proportions have always had a magical association. They are absolutely unique. Answers to the question about the essence of art have been the touchstone of philosophy. / Odd figures for the male. Even for the female. / Proportions are common to all the arts.

Pythagoras discovered the relationship between music and painting.

ARCHITECTURAL PRINCIPLES

Leonardo accepted that music and painting had their essence in common ... harmonies, proportion, and went out of his way to point out the superiority of painting.

In the Italian Renaissance the knowledge of proportions was an accepted fact. Not only specialists, artists who obviously suggest a mathematical certainty like Piero or Ucello or Alberti, but even other most unlikely artists.

In 1534 the Doge of Venice laid the foundation of a new church San Francesco della Vigna, but arguments arose about the proportions of the plan, and a Franciscan monk Giorgi was commissioned to write a memorandum on the proportions.

Three men were consulted about the memorandum as experts in different fields. A Humanist Fortunio Spira, an architect Serlio and the painter <u>Titian</u>.

NOTES ON PRINCIPLES OF PALLADIO'S ARCHITECTURE
Palladio's size of rooms which might equally well go for size of canvas.

A division. / Eight feet eight inches. / Pythagorean. [Platonic] philosophy of numbers. / Poem on proportions of a courtyard. / From Trisino. / L'Italia Liberata. / Vitruvius. / Alberti.

·

Palladio: 'Beauty will result from the beautiful form and from the correspondence of the whole to the parts, of the parts amongst themselves, and of these again to the whole; so that the structures may appear an entire and complete body wherein each member agrees with the other and all members are necessary for the accomplishment of the building.'

·

Palladio measured the antique Roman ruins. / The particular outline inherent in architecture. The possibility of materialising in space the 'certain truth' of mathematics. / Ratios. Harmonies.

·

Photographs of classical basilicas. Renaissance temples. House of Raphael and Bramante's Palazzo Chiericati façade in terms of a Roman Forum.

There is no such thing as originality.

·

Mathematics has its life from the intellect; and these arts which are founded on numbers, geometry and other mathematical disciplines, have [appealness] and in there lies the dignity of architecture. About Barbaro.

.

Alberti says, on Vitruvius: 'Beauty consists of the rational integrations of the proportions of all the parts of the building, in such a way that every part has its absolutely fixed size and shape, and nothing could be added or taken away without destroying the harmony of the whole ... Music is geometry translated into sound.'

.

... clean rythm ... the relationship of mass to space is in proportion, the eye [transmutes] to the brain co-ordinated sensations and the mind derives from these satisfactions of a high order: this is architecture.

.

Palladio's [?]: 1. Circular ○ / 2. Square □ / 3. Diagonal of the square √2:1 4. Square + ⅓ 3:4 / 5. Square + ½ 2:3 / 6. Square ⅔ 3:5 / 7. Two squares 1:2

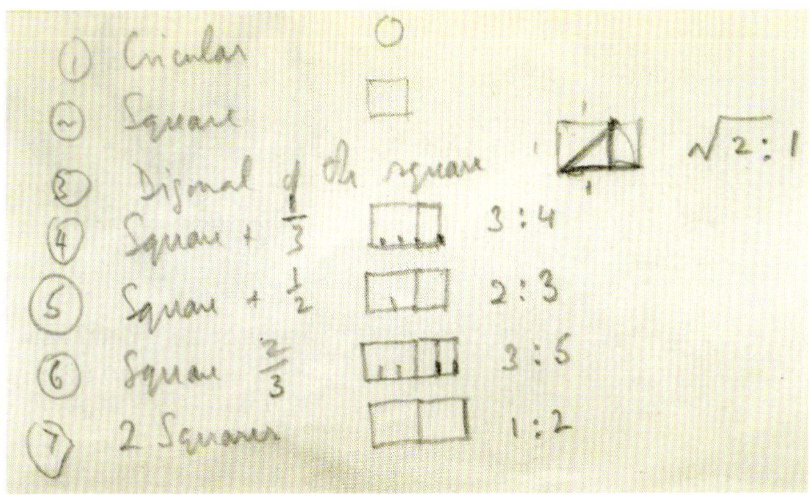

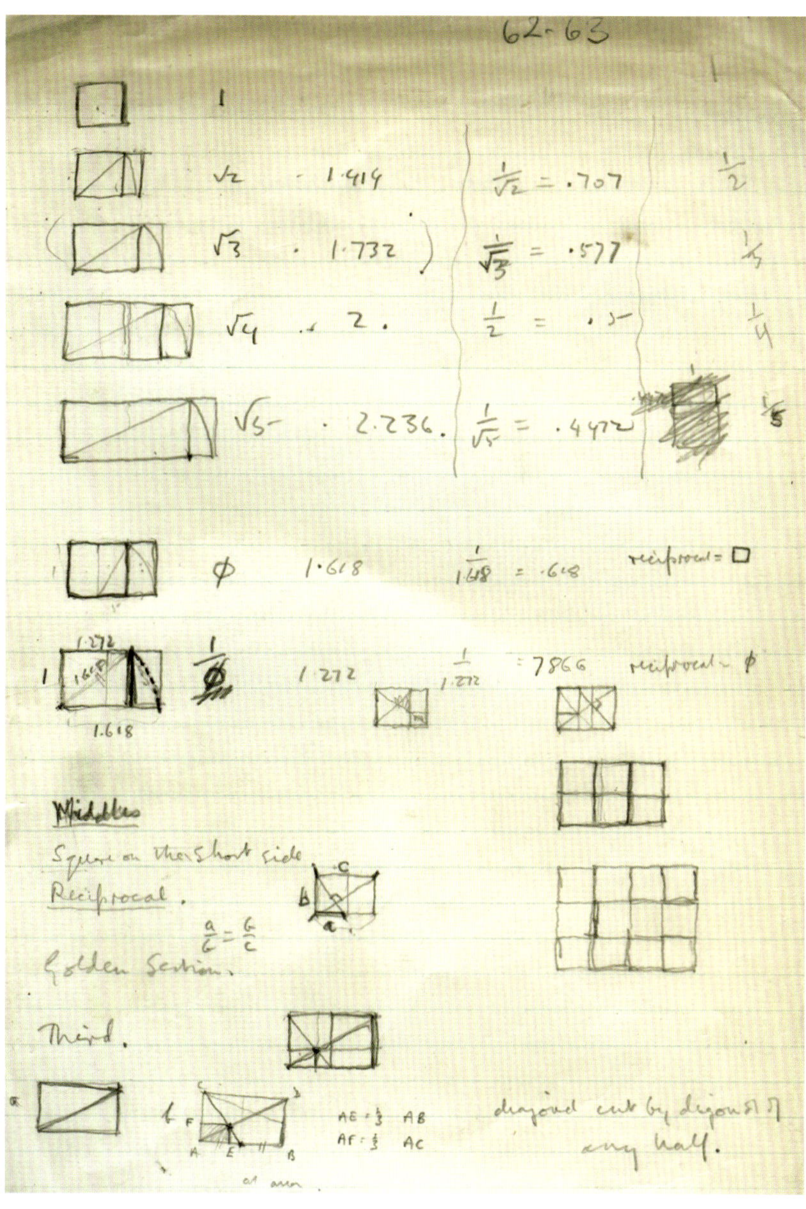

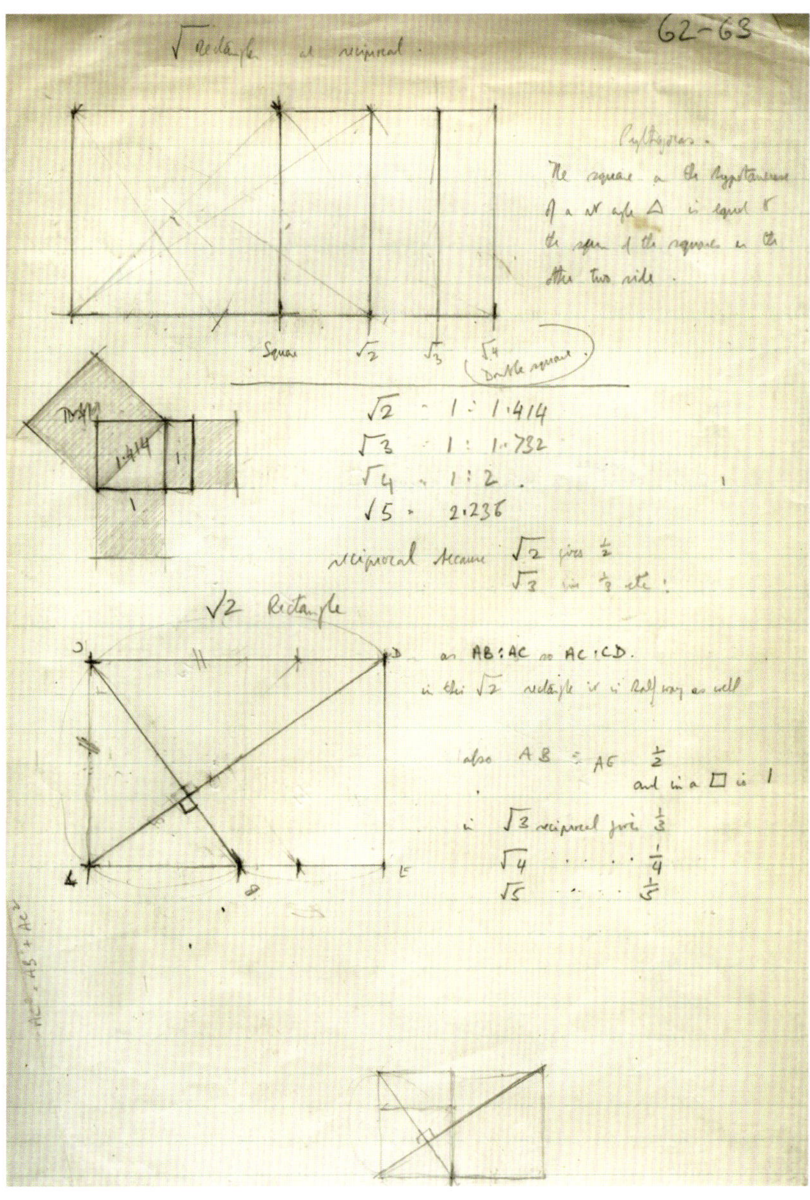
√ Rectangle & reciprocal.
62-63
Pythagoras.
The square on the hypotenuse of a rt angle △ is equal to the sum of the squares on the other two sides.
Square   √2   √3   √4 (Double square)
√2 = 1 : 1·414
√3 = 1 : 1·732
√4 = 1 : 2
√5 = 2·236
reciprocal because √2 gives ½
√3 gives ⅓ etc.
√2 Rectangle
as AB : AC = AC : CD.
in this √2 rectangle it is half way as well
also AB = AE ½
and in a ▢ it is 1
in √3 reciprocal gives ⅓
√4 . . . . . ¼
√5 . . . . . ⅕

MUSIC AND ARCHITECTURE
Severini A and A 438

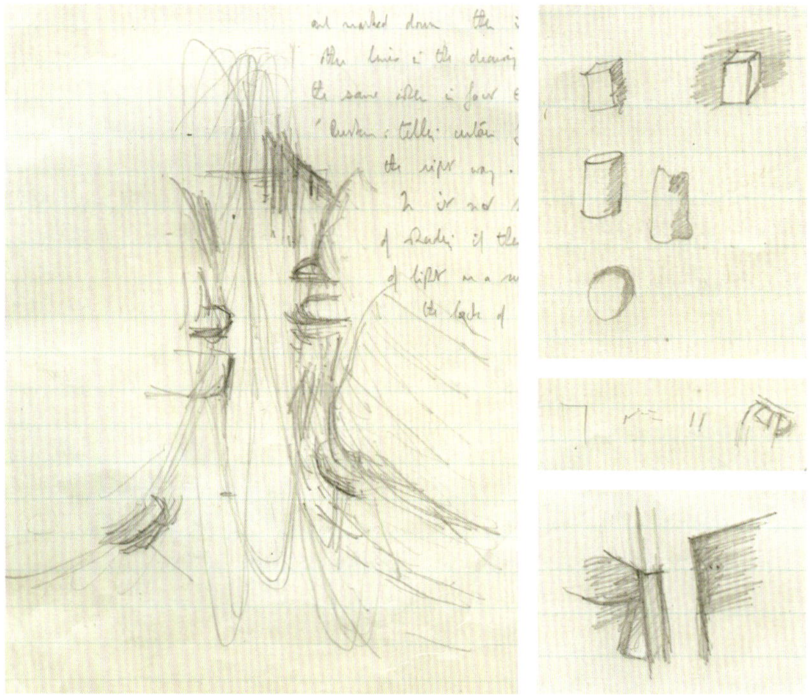

Pythagorean musical [scale]. If you have two strings, one half as long as another, when they are vibrated the pitch of one will be an octave above the other and similarly halved in length again the difference will be a fifth, and in the relation of 3:4 a fourth, 1:2:3:4.

If the length of the string are 2:3 the difference in pitch will be a fifth. Diapente. As 3:4 a fourth diatessaron. The Greek musical system 1:2:3:4. Octave fifth and fourth and octave plus a fifth 1:2:3 and two octaves 1:2:4.

Plato in Timaeus explained cosmic order and harmony 1, 2, 4, 8 and 1, 3, 9, 27.

[is] a Lambda   1

       2   3

    4   9

   8   27   or   1, 2, 3, 4, 8, 9, 27.

PARALLELS BETWEEN VISUAL ART AND MUSIC

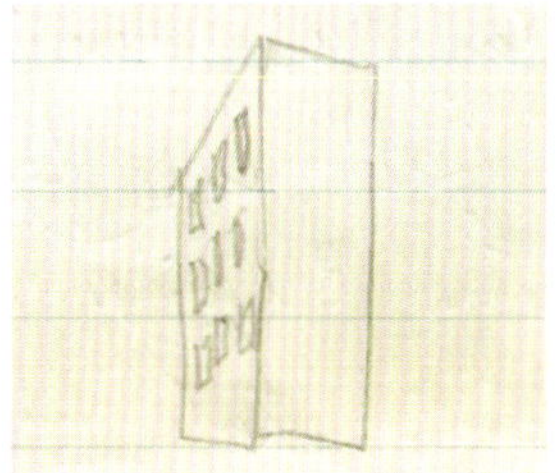

A length of a string vibrated.
A string half as long as another will vibrate exactly an octave above.
A piece of [foolscap] is a ∅.
[Seurat] Mondrian, Le Corbusier.

ARCHITECTURAL PRINCIPLES IN THE AGE OF HUMANISM

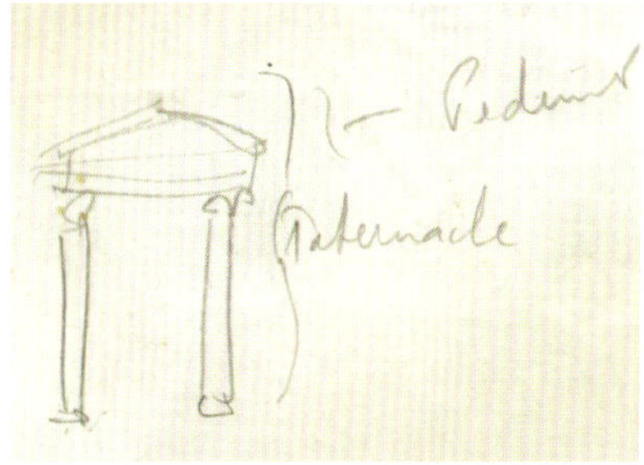

[Vitruvian] all important postulates of symmetrical, which is the fixed mathematical [routes] of the parts to each other and to the whole.

Modula. / Three is the first real number. Pythagoras. Beginning middle and end. Trinity.

DIVISION OR MULTIPLICATION FOUND IN REAL LIFE

Look along a roof line. Divisions of a window pane. Pipes on the outside of houses [and] windows. Chimney stacks. Television [masts].

ROUNDS

Alberti says: 'Nature herself enjoys the round forms above all others as is proved by her own creations such as the globe. The stars. The trees. The animals and their nests and many other things.'

The academic tradition is made up. From the School of Paris painting is decorative. Perhaps similar to Venetian painting. The supreme made up picture is Abstract Expressionism, Tachism. Perhaps made up painting accounts for most pictures. Objective painters are rare and perhaps the interest is alive in only very few artists.

REGULAR SOLIDS, SHAPES FROM CHEMISTRY

Draw lines on blackboard bases.

Draw plane after plane – in succession. Moving from the objects to the board to the next object hardly aware that you are moving from one object to another. Describe a sequence of planes even if not a succession of objects. Treat the outlines (the lines of the far boundaries of the planes) as just that, and with no more special attention. The base to be another plane determined only by its angle to the adjacent plane of the object.

Draw these successions of planes truthfully and with that single minded concentration without which you will never be able to call yourselves artists. 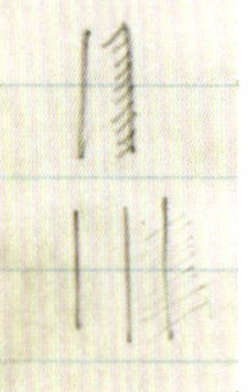

All faces similar. The arrangement around the vertices the same. In a cube three faces meet in a point.

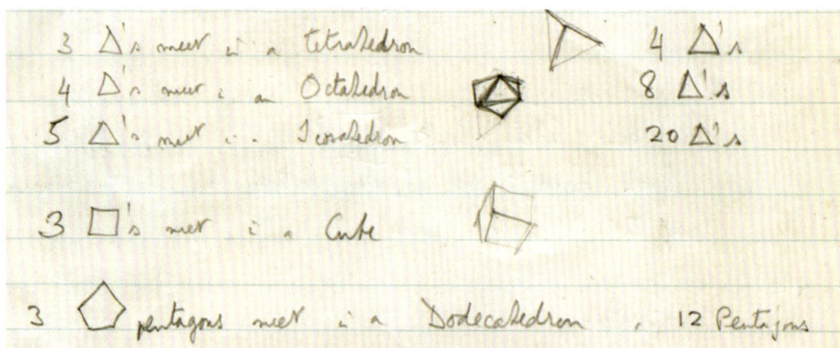

Three triangles meet in a tetrahedron (four triangles). Four triangles meet in a octahedron (eight triangles). Five triangles meet in a icosahedron (twenty triangles). Three squares meet in a cube. Three pentagons meet in a dodecahedron (twelve pentagons). All regular solids inscribed in a sphere. Certain crystals form perfect cubes and dodecahedrons.

40 SOLIDS FROM CHEMISTRY

Solid objects. / Regular geometrical arranged on white paper. / [Arrastes]. Lines to show the changes within the outline. / Tetrahedron. Octahedron. Icosahedron. Cube. Pentagon. Dodecahedron.

APPLES

The apples seem round but after you have looked at them for a few minutes or have attempted to trace their boundaries you will find that the outline changes its direction at various quite well defined points and there mark the vertisces of the planes.

Within the apple you can usually find some speck or blemish to help you find your way across the form.

I should like you to recognise the apples as some sort of irregular solid made up of a succession of planes.

.

Explaining the surface within the contour. The uniqueness of the boundary of one object to another disappeared. The lines within the shapes or explaining the outline were the same. They marked a change of plane.

Nevertheless these were not diagrammatic marks. Each line could be accounted for, marking a ridge on the limits of two planes. But if there is not a clear division, if the surface slowly changes direction, if we wish to explain this and if all the marks in the drawing are still to be accounted for on the objects, in this case apples, we have to make use of the effect of light and shade.

As an object turns away from the light it gets darker. So by making an area of a surface darker it will seem to be turning away from the light. Warning that this does not mean copying the light and dark patches. That is a tonal study and something different from explaining the shape.

There would not be very much to drawing if it was only a matter of drawing elevations. Drawing would become a matter of skill and dexterity and would be a craft that one could learn. The predetermined drawing. Right to how a drawing looks. How can you get out of this repetitive situation. Apply a principal. The unrecognisable marks.

APPLES AND SKULLS

Yesterday I asked you to start from the middle of the objects. From the vertices back, explaining plane by plane until you have described the scene.

Today I ask you to consider these apples as subtle modifications of the geometrical solids.

To describe their bulk you will no longer be able to grasp at the edges but will have to consider how their shape can best be described by using the effect of light. Make an area darker to show it is at a different angle to its neighbour.

Draw from the middle making up nothing. Find a blemish, a bird peck and move to the next one describing the surface as it moves away from you towards the boundaries.

Lines following the form more or less (Ruskin). / Description of the base and environment. / Size and use of paper.

Beware the shading up, the process drawing. Each line is drawn – perhaps lightly. Perhaps to explain no more than the lack of light on the surface of the object.

How much of this explanation seems necessary will vary with each of you, Cézanne was sparing, explained the situation at the crucial points and lights and left the rest. Rembrandt perhaps influenced by his experience as an etcher used all the range that lines could give him.

.

Have clearly in your heads the distance you have carved back from the front of your page. The distance as a positively considered aspect of your drawing and part of the essential description of the object.

Leoanardo said: 'Empty space begins where the object ends. Where empty space ends the object begins and where the object ends emptiness begins'.

Describe by your awareness the empty space. Almost as if you were considering the space as a cast of the object. Try to imagine the surrounding air of the skulls and apples as a body with substance and the objects as hollows or spaces in that body.

Or imagine the space and objects like a large piece of gruyère cheese, the cheese being the space, the bubbles in the cheese being where the objects lie.

Or imagine a photographic negative, the white spaces black, the black white, imagine it in three dimensions. The objects as interruptions to the three-dimensional blackness.

So carve back from the surface of your page from that part of the object which is nearest to you.

<u>Order of drawing</u>. Nearer objects first. Border round the page. Penetrating, describing the space.

.

Cézanne: 'Empty space begins where the object ends, where empty space ends the object begins and where the object ends emptiness begins.' *Ordeal of Paul Cézanne*. Rewald (author on Impressionists).

.

Explain the shape of the receding space and the objects. <u>Use no outlines</u>. No special continuous line to demark one thing from another. All the lines on your page should be the same. Explanations of form.

SHADING

The pencilling goes on the parts in shadow – to show that there parts are turned from the light – but you can imagine a plane tilted to catch the light but far back from the picture plane. Suppose you do a drawing with no outlines. Working back from that part that is nearest to you.

The shade goes on first and simply marks its limit and the edge of the form with a boundary line. Explanation not only of the forms but of the space.

The solid objects leaving a solid space. Abrupt as if you could take the objects out of the space and leave the space shaped by their forms.

Space as flat shapes left over – the surrounding area, the space between.

Space as distance, objects far and near. The distance from you measured by imaginary rods from your eyes to the objects.

.

<u>Space as the cast of the objects</u>. Caves are in the dark and projections catch the light. So we associate darkness with recession and light with projection.

If we darken a part of the page it will appear a different distance from your eye, compared to the rest of the page usually in this context it will appear farther back than the white part of the page.

How does Giacometti deal with shading? Lines of dimension which also simulates light. Lines within the contour. If the external lines are drawn from observation and marked down then it is inconsistent that other lines in the drawing should appear to do the same when in fact they do not.

Ruskin: '... telling certain facts not in quite the right way. Is it not better that the lines of shading, if they indicate the lack of light on a surface only represent the lack of light.'

·

All the lines in drawing are conventional marks used to make clear what you mean and all the lines should mean something. The idea that shading is carving back from the surface of the paper.

The light gives the planes an order. / Lines are used where the form alters. / The line defines limits of the shape or divisions within it. / Other lines which do not rest on boundaries, divisions or marks can be used to more fully explain the shape of the object.

But suppose the objects to be described are not all the same distance from you. Then what is the nature of the page in relationship to the things that are seen? The paper becomes an imaginary three-dimensional area – a white mist close yet capable of being penetrated to a great depth.

·

The phenomenon.

Flat things appear smaller as they are farther away from the eye. Up, down, sideways and farther off. By reproducing this phenomena we can give a description of the order of the objects in space. The larger objects appear nearer than the same object recognised farther away. / The same <u>space</u> appears smaller further away. / The streets at night. The street lamps and the tail lights of cars.

·

Describing the volume of the room.

It is perhaps impossible to draw anything unless one has seen a drawing. The plumb line and the horizontal brought some connection between real life and the page. I do not think the half made up, half objective picture is possible today.

Work hard, you are not dilettantes.

ON DRAWING

These classes are concerned with the problem of drawing things. This is not at all as straightforward as it may seem.

We learn the language of drawing mainly by imitation of drawings. Or anyway other pictures, other translations of the real world into marks on a flat surface and gradually we acquire our way of drawing and are able to make recognisable likenesses of things.

You all have done a good deal of drawing and are all able to make very adequate likenesses. It is at this stage that it becomes very difficult to draw what you see. Faced with a familiar object you apply the familiar drawing, modifying it here and there as the case may be. You must understand that this does not mean you necessarily draw or paint worse. I am not concerned with art, only with the much narrower problem of objective drawing. I do think that it does become increasingly difficult to see and to draw just what you see, the more facility you acquire for doing a competent drawing.

During this term I shall bring to you a few of the problems concerned with describing objects by drawing them. This is by no means an exact science. For instance it is impossible scientifically, that is to say reasonably, to reproduce a spherical surface on a flat sheet of paper. You have all seen the problem in the hands of the map makers and you will remember Mercator's projection where the relative directions remain true but the areas are distorted. In a map of the world, Canada and Greenland have a much greater area than they should have in proportion to the rest of the world.

Perhaps I should apologise for making you spend a term considering such elementary things and certainly you will have heard before much that I am going to say, but I believe it is not a waste of your time, although that mainly depends on you.

These classes do not set out to give you useful tips on how to draw. Nor do they lay down any particular way of drawing that may find favour in the school. If you look at the drawings hanging in the passages you will see that it is not any particular style of drawing that is encouraged in the school. These classes are entirely my concern – in fact they are exactly my concern with the problem of drawing what I see. But I do try to substantiate what I present to you by referring to the writing of various artists.

I shall be very surprised if you agree with all I say but I am not laying down a cannon for your own art. When you are in this room I should like you to put to one side your <u>own</u> artistic interests or if that seems to compromise you, then rather consider these classes as some sort of party game. Like all games there are rules. Each day I lay down the rules and you must keep to them. If you do not then you will be wasting your time and you have little time to waste.

Perhaps you are surprised that you will have to spend so much of your time drawing this term. But drawing with its obvious limitations has, because of those limitations, certain advantages over painting. Within its limits it is more exciting and it arrives quicker at the crux of the problem. This school is perhaps most famous for its drawing.

.

As Michelangelo said: 'Let this be plain to all. Design or as it is called by another name drawing constitutes the fountainhead and substance of painting, sculpture and architecture.'

.

Explain exactly how you want the drawing done. Without so much pre-calculating as to hide the intention. I think you should draw as you see, it is more exciting.

Drawings have tension. / Drawing is a deliberate gesture.

.

Paul Klee: '... a point shifting its position forward. Nothing in speed. Those who can draw slowest can also draw fastest. An active line is a walk, moving freely, without a goal. A walk for a walk's sake. The mobility agent <u>is a point shifting its position forward</u>.'

.

That drawing and painting are the same. / Familiarity of the pencil and the strangeness of the brush. / Writing and painting.

.

'Again if you wish to mount to the top of an edifice you must go up step by step; otherwise it will be impossible to reach the top.' (Leonardo, boys learning to paint page.)

[Courbet] to [Bruyas] in 1869 after 20 years painting he had executed 2000 important canvases Cézanne ... Vollard's shirt front. Bach said the only difference between him and other musicians was that he worked harder.

PAINTING CLASS
Cylindrical object against dark background. Bottom half against light background. Colour of the shadow in the object.

Using bright colours unmixed. He which aspires to spirited qualities must have a basis of strong colours, beautiful blue, beautiful red, beautiful yellow colour, so as to satisfy the fundamental desires of our senses.

.

The training of the artist: There is household decoration, there is sentimentality, how are you going to learn to steer your course.

.

Each brushstroke should be a living idea. European idea of the 'touch of the genius'. Dürer. / Handwriting of an artist. Van Gogh. Kokoschka.

NATURAL FORMS
Hard and soft forms. / Matisse via Besson. / Painting. / Oranges. Lemons. Grapefruit. / A cast torso wrapped in a sheet. / A tree trunk for sculpture? / A flint or two. / Balloon with water.

.

The classes in touch with everyday objects. Especially growing things. / Deliberate gestures. Considering the pattern on the sheet.

TONE DRAWING
The mystery of parcels and what they might contain. / Wrapped casts, skulls, apples, eggs.

.

Big things to be reduced to a small size. Lost in the middle.

.

Marks and tone. How to draw. Free standing. Difference of scale.

/ Taking first things first. Children's marks. Precision. / Saying exactly what you mean. Exactly. Getting through the veil of convention.

.

Lines. / Angle of relationship. / Spaces. / Cumulative drawing. / Beware of line between, stands in the way of the reaction to the look of the thing.

.

Dürer: 'Without proportion no figure can even be perfect, even though it is made with all possible diligence … If on the contrary, it has its right measurement, it cannot be condemned by anyone, even though it is executed quite simply.'

Mondrian: '… the balanced relation is the present representation of universality, of the harmony and unity which are inherent characteristics of the mark. Yes all things are part of a whole. Each part receives its visual value form the whole, and the whole receives its visual value from the parts. Everything is constituted by relative and reciprocity … Colour exists only through another colour, dimension is defined by another dimension; there is no position except of opposition to another position. That is why I say relation is the principal thing. One thing can only be known through something else.'

REGULAR SOLIDS
Solid geometrical objects and cooking apples.

Surfaces turned from the light get darker. / Similar brightness means similar angle to the light. / Making dark one side with tone may no more describe the shape of an apple than making the relief deep. A lump of clay is not a description of an apple – a flat drawing may be a better description.

.

Apples and the solids.

The middle. / The rocks. Do not put down any mark that you cannot account for. The surfaces. Principles of shading.

.

Relationship of solids to the apples.

Danger of tonal illusion, local colour. Painting with a pencil that the lines and the tone are showing the same thing. The change of surface. / In an attempt to show the change of surface both lines and tone will be used. And at the same time. It is never a question of drawing the outline and filling in.

.

Articulated lines.

Drinking straws. Lining paper. Charcoal. Dip the straws in black paint so that they more clearly resemble the twigs. / Twigs taped back flat onto the walls. Precision, not natural history. / Enclosures. Twigs laced together.

.

Mondrian. Pasmore. Victor Pasmore. English artist stages to abstraction.

.

Contiguous shapes: Expanding. First shape. Second shape. Common boundary and form. Third shape that encloses them both. Shapes under tension.

CONTINUOUS LINE

An infinite number of positions. A trail. A wake, a ship's wake. Time. / You walk in circles. The arms and hand movements in arcs. / Force lines. Children's circular lines. / There are two parts. Making the walk and recording it.

.

The objective drawings are descriptions of the line and a description of a thing is never the thing itself.

The description is not an impression. It will usually be a simplification of the object but the nature of the description line will be more complicated.

.

Desmond Morris (anthropologist).

Congo 1½ yr old chimpanzee, first drawing: 'I held out the pencil. His curiosity led him towards it and gently I placed his fingers around it and rested the point on the card. Then I let go. As I did so, he moved his [arm] a little and then stopped. He stared at the card. Something odd was coming out of the end of the pencil. It was Congo's first line ...'

You can make a likeness of things seen by seeing them in terms that are possible to draw (that are compatible with paper and pencil): you can elect to see the objects in flowing rhythm because it is possible to draw lines suggestive of flowing rhythm on the paper or you can see the objects in terms of verticals and horizontals or the reciprocating relationship of lines at the other angles.

With this distinction in mind: a. Make a drawing of your shoes; b. Make a drawing of the matchboxes.

Although you should make two drawings to show you understand the different way things may be drawn, do not feel hurried; draw at your own pace, even if this means only one drawing will be completed.

.

Drawing the likeness. Composition.

'To draw a likeness is to make an order and to appreciate an order is to compose'. / Sheriden. Relationship being the common feature of likeness and composition. / Collier. Drawing a likeness is a matter of finding a composition which is already there. / J. Jones ... to show them off to the best advantage. / La Rue. Composing is adjusting. / Warre: 'But as I have learned from the first drawing lecture, sometimes, if the objects are drawn really truthfully they gain a satisfactory composition of their own. They gradually arrange themselves as did the dots ...'

.

Picture contrivances.

From notion about picture making. Flat. Straight off marks will seem as much furniture as the branches and set piece trees of the seventeenth century.

.

Implied three-dimensional composition. When a square becomes a window instead of a square. / As if the face of the picture was tipped backwards.

Try slide of two-dimensional picture and Rubens Leningrad landscape. Pastoral landscape with Rainbow. / Veronese. / Front to back and (otherway) Claude.

Lengths are implied by perspective description. Scale. / Almost a sculptor's language.

Pegging down a space. Taking you for a walk here and there, through and around. Travel down the road and are halted by a cow. You travel far, you go a great distance but cover little canvas.

.

The size of the canvas is not fixed. You may change the relative size of the canvas but you may not change the relative proportion of things. Why not? Because if you do, you change their identity; if you wish to describe a girl's face then it is that identity that you wish to describe. It will not describe her to say she has a long thin face if she has proportions usually associated (by the ratio) with fat faced people.

But the terms of a canvas remain its terms. When it is done. There will be a middle and an edge.

Try out the proportion on a piece of cartridge paper. / Panels on a door. Window frames. / The door. The paving stones.

.

Cut out postcards to varying proportions. Pasted on black paper. Cut out square of PC's build up rectangles. Practice drawing accurately certain special rectangles. Acquire a knowledge of rectangles. Recognition.

Composition of position. Position in a rectangle. Rhythm. Measure. / All have an idea of what the drawing should look like. Why not let the idea make the drawing. A direction in style.

.

The purpose of schemata was to enable the painter to draw the <u>general</u>. In front of an object the painter can recognise a schemata particular to his and the objects relationship. The schemata in both cases reduces the real life object into terms that are comprehensible in two dimensions. In the first case to make some marks that are recognisable as some other thing and in the second case to translate the appearance of a real thing into a the terms of some marks.

The schema of perspective, of anatomy.

TOWARDS A NEW ARCHITECTURE – LE CORBUSIER
The establishment of a standard is developed by organizing rational elements, following a line of direction equally rational.

The form and appearance are in no way preconceived, they are a result; they may have a strange look at first sight. Ader made a 'Bat', but it did not fly; Wright and Farman set themselves the problem of sustaining solid bodies in air, the result was jarring and disconcerting, but it flew. The standard has been fixed. Practical results followed.

FROM LIFE. TWO MODELS POSED AGAINST A BLACK BACKGROUND

Outstretched legs at ease. Arms resting on two easels. / From life. The first living thing. / Preconceptions. / Movement of the object. / Outline. / Back view. Front view.

CURVES

How can you account for a curve.

The curved line. / Perfect curves, imperfect are not curves. / Very few. The mind can't stand the right description of a perfect curve.

Nor for that matter of a straight which no more exists in actual appearance than the perfect curve.

Spring. Bending. Bow. Rhythm. / French curves. Fair curves? / Female. Waves. Boats. Space. Hanging string. / The spiral. A graph through positions. / Flow. / Currents. String. Let fall freely. But the free trail has been dealt with. / The positions in sequence are not in any one direction. / Hair. / Strength, arch.

The circle. The arc. The articulated line becomes the wiggle. / Canes with pins.

Aircraft view of rivers. A river is a big curve. It flows and pushes against the bank. Curves in three dimensions. / Making fair curves. Cane. / Positions of articulation in a fair curve.

A circle is a straight line of infinite [radius]? Fair curves, from french curve most distinguishable.

The position of change of direction becomes indistinguishable. The fair curve is the most economic joining of four positions (that are not able to be circumscribed by a circle nor is a straight line) so that the exact positions are no longer apparent.

<u>Extracting position</u>. By distance from each other. Interval. By angle from each other. Some angles have particular associations. A right angle.

Some directions of position are special. / The horizontal and vertical direction.

See and appreciate the positions and draw what you can see. (Draw the positions you can see.) / Oranges rolled onto the floor describe their positions. Landscape. / Close up one each. Someone lying on the floor amongst the oranges.

·

Shading. Elevation and plan. Front to back. / Oranges. The form. / Articulate the paper. Simulate the relief proportionally. Crumpled page, imitation of crumpled page. Do again.

Drawing round things. Drawing around each other and attempting to get as like and far from pencil as possible. Stencil.

·

How to draw from photographs. Photographs from newspapers.

Drawing as an artists recorded gesture. How the mark is conditioned by the sheet of paper. Here, there. Middle. Square.

Golden Section. Balance. Distance. / The sheet of paper. The field. The message to be got on it./ Rectangular. / Amorphous. / Making sheets of paper of different dimension. / Cut out. Torn.

The choice of the connection of one form to another or to another.

CONTIGUOUS SHAPES

On brown paper, black paper, newspaper ...

Try clothes pressed large, or small shapes, and really reset to this, before should be silhouette? / And then double silhouette? Contiguous shape from magazine illustrations.

Draw shape from. <u>Cut shape</u> from. Draw shape. Stick on. Next to silhouette where the process is exactly the other way round. From the naturalistic representation to the shapes of art. From the cast shadow shape of art the naturalistic information of likeness.

Tracing pictures. Shapes. / Drawing round. Contiguous shapes. / Shapes. Clothes. Try and draw a shape that doesn't look like anything but a shape. Leaves. / Tracing or making with cut out paper. / Make a big shape. Different creative shapes. / <u>Your own shape</u>. Large cut out paper shapes. / Puddles. Blots. Pancakes.

.

<u>Draw a shape and 1) pass to neighbour</u>. <u>They draw it</u>.

2) Draw a copy of the shape full size. Trace it.

Then draw a shape pass it on. Shapes generally became bigger more complicated bulkier, lost their particular characteristic. Possibly eventually all the shapes would have come out the same.

.

Developing shape. Made paper cut outs.

Drawing in coloured chalk. One colour for each shape and each combination. Reproductions of pictures. Ensure that the outline of the shape is drawn where it comes to the edge of the paper (in the same way that the rest of the outline is drawn). Do not draw in pencil first. Draw the lines over each other when they coincide, not alongside. Draw, if on the same scale, on large pieces of paper. / Giorgione. 'Dresden Venus'. Titian 'Holy Family'. Munch 'The Day After.'

.

Make full sized stencils of each other. / Find out how much of real life can be trapped this way. / Semi-mechanical ways of making the record was tracing.

.

Draw from photographs in lines. Actual size. Make tracing. / Difference of the free hand line and the even directionless traced line. The two side by side.

Drawing is management. Changing the area of a patch of colour is drawing. Marking where the area is, is drawing the maximum area.

THE AMATEUR AND THE PROFESSIONAL

The amateur tries to do the prodigious – through innocence.

The professional learns to take the calculated risk, is fearful to the degree that he is knowledgeable. So as he knows more he attempts less. Nor through lack of ambition but through increase of knowledge. The still life does not require the whole supper table, a simple egg cup will do.

The professional has to do it well. The pro does it economically and well – he has to do it another day. The amateur is (strategist?) with everything – idea – material – energy waste and mess. Probably mostly with idea and often misunderstanding that the intention has to be in paint. The professional energetically, worryingly, cunningly bad temperedly, reduces the problem to a possibility it should be possible.

PROJECT WITH COMPOSER JAMES ILIFF

Reading from left to right. / Some things set up their rhythm in relation to and against something. Echo with its own rhythm.

One lives from past to future. / Some marks darker (louder) than others. / Red, yellow, blue, black, white. White, yellow, red, blue, black.

Rhythm is not necessarily wallpaper rhythm nor rock but you can play the flower pot or hear Big Ben chiming. / Difference but similarity: a great [many] positions, a few. / Exactitude if not exact nor rhythmic.

Play the drawings each person in a row. / Seeing music everywhere. (Hearing pictures.) / Squared paper 2's 3's 5's 8. Golden Mean. / Fibonacci series.

Varied tins to bring. Milk bottles. Stick, rulers. Tools. / [Spanners], knives and forks. Hard backed books. Boxes. Artificial contrivance of objects on a table.

One pattern. / Two rhythm.

Played are instruments. / And like this only with different set of instruments and different colours. / Four different sets. The different colours for the different [sort] of instruments but nearer the top of the page higher. / Rhythm, beat, pattern (static, regular continuous). Irregular but has correspondences.

The no-mans land between music and painting. / Not necessarily flowing rhythms. / Mondrian. / But not to let it slip one way or another. / Explain difference between.

Time. Pattern and rhythm is unappreciated repetition. / Explain on table with wooden bricks. / They make drawings of position and interval.

They ask James to explain what he has done. / And explain the similarities and differences of music.

They make pieces for percussion with pencils, glasses, plates, coloured pencils, different colours, different sets, with things arranged on the table.

Play the scene. / Arranged in line from left to right. / Simpler intervals in music. Reading pictures from left to right.

James plays his pieces.

MUSICAL COMPOSITION

The [deliberate] [ordering] of sounds. Put one noise against another. / Traditional composition and stopping places. Cadences. / Masculine ending. Dominant [tonic]. / Feminine ending. Sub dominant [tonic]. / Stopping places, interrupted cadences. Half close ends [on] the dominant binary or [ternerary] form. / A B time / A B A (4 far [phrase] [?] by 4 ba [phrase])

Originally when you had to take a breath. Poetry and music. / The leap, you should either shorten or come down because this is [expected]. / The four voices, soprano, alto, tenor, bass.

ACKNOWLEDGEMENTS

I WOULD LIKE TO THANK SCOTT PURDIN FOR HIS GREAT generosity and enthusiasm for this book, without whom it would perhaps never have been published. His involvement and genuine passion for Patrick's writings and painting has been the driving force behind the whole project.

Sincere thanks to Christopher Moock who took a huge amount of trouble to write a serious and very well researched introduction to the book.

Also I would like to thank Samantha Combs who worked hard and patiently transcribing all of Patrick's notes, written in a tiny and almost indecipherable hand, not an easy task!

Grateful thanks also to all at Sansom & Co., in particular to Gemma Brace for her great work pulling the book together and working with me to get the writings to a clear and well ordered form, and to Ian Parfitt for his careful attention to the elegant and intelligent design. Also huge thanks to Paul Deaton whose profound understanding of Patrick's writing and discussions with me on the book were invaluable.

I would also like to thank Andrew Warrington who was a huge support during the long period when I was immersed in the book, and for his work on scanning Patrick's drawings and taking the photographs of Patrick and his work. I would also wish to thank Robert Dukes for the many patient hours of discussion and trawling through a great many photographs of work and finding pertinent information with me.

It has been an enormous pleasure for me to see this book published and for people to be able to access the thinking behind the teaching and painting of Patrick George.

EDITOR'S NOTE

THE VARIOUS TEXTS WITHIN THIS BOOK ARE COLLATED from Patrick George's extensive writings, including transcriptions from notebooks relating to both his personal painting practice and position as a lecturer (and later Professor) at The Slade School of Art.

The diary, teaching and lecture notes have been transcribed specifically for this publication. Wherever possible, with the exception of changes to grammar, punctuation and capitalisation for consistency and comprehension, these notes have been left untouched. However, due to the fragmentary nature of George's notes in 'Notes on painting', 'Lecture notes' and 'Teaching notes' some editorial changes have been made to paragraphs, layout and structure to help with clarity (whilst endeavouring to maintain the poeticism of the original text).

Throughout the book where words appear underlined this is a reflection of the original markings made by George within his notes or in the original publications. Words struck through in the original text but included in transcription have been removed except where they aid comprehension. Where necessary pronouns and prepositions have been added (and removed) to aid clarity. All quotes remain in their original transcribed form and subsequently reflect George's recollection rather than the original source.

ABOUT THE AUTHORS

SUSAN ENGLEDOW

Susan Engledow (b. 1947) was born in Surrey. She was taught art by David Hepher before studying at The Slade School of Fine Art (1965–71) under the Professorship of Sir William Coldstream. Here, she was also taught by Patrick George, Frank Auerbach and Euan Uglow, and from 1965 onwards sat for several portraits by George. From 1971 she taught painting at The Heatherley School of Fine Art becoming the Director of the Diploma in Portraiture in 1994, a post she held until 2014. During this period she spent a teaching sabbatical at the University of New York, Stonybrook, Long Island. Engledow worked and lived in London (with her husband the physicist Leonardo Castillejo before his death) before moving to Suffolk with George, who remained her partner until his death in 2016. She now lives and works in London.

CHRISTOPHER MOOCK

Christopher Moock (b. 1959) is a painter and art historian. He has a BA in Painting from The Slade School of Fine Art (1977–81) and an MA in History of Art from Birkbeck, University of London (1988–90). He teaches painting and art history at The Heatherley School of Fine Art, Chelsea, with an emphasis on portraiture, and lectures at Birkbeck, University of London, specialising in seventeenth century art. His academic work is underpinned by his practical experience of painting, and his portrait paintings have been exhibited at The National Portrait Gallery. His publications include articles on Baroque art and contemporary painting.

PATRICK GEORGE

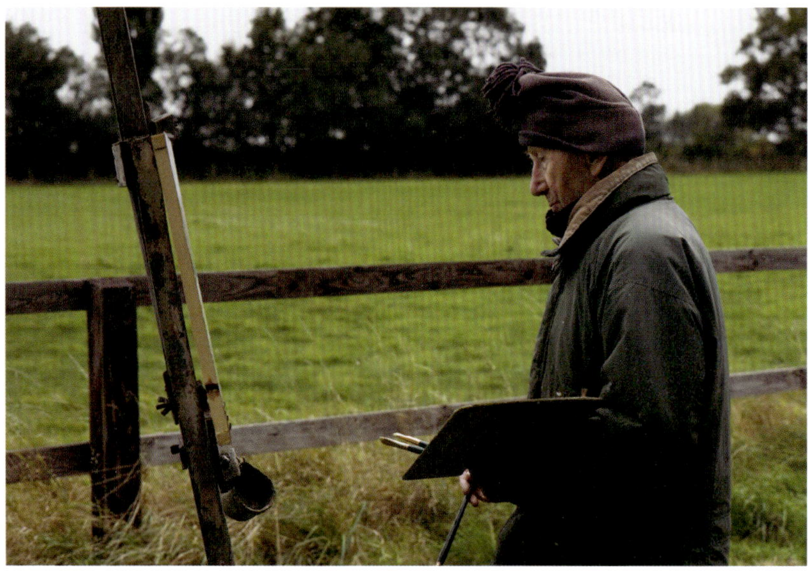

Painting in the Suffolk landscape, 2012 © Andrew Warrington

PATRICK HERBERT GEORGE (1923–2016) WAS BORN IN Wilmslow and educated at The Downs Prep School, near Malvern (where he was taught by Maurice Field and W.H. Auden) and at Bryanston School in Dorset. His studies at Edinburgh School of Art (1941–42) were interrupted by World War Two, during which he served in the Royal Navy and was in command of a landing craft during the D-Day Landings. Following the War he studied at Camberwell School of Art (1946–49) where he was taught by Victor Pasmore and Sir William Coldstream, members of The Euston Road School. In 1949 he began teaching at The Slade School of Fine Art, spending a year abroad teaching at The Nigerian College of Art in Zaria from 1959–60. He was made Director of The Slade (known as The Slade Professor) from 1985–88. Throughout his life he lived and painted in London and Suffolk and spent the last years of his life in Great Saxham, near Bury St Edmunds. He died on 23rd April 2016.